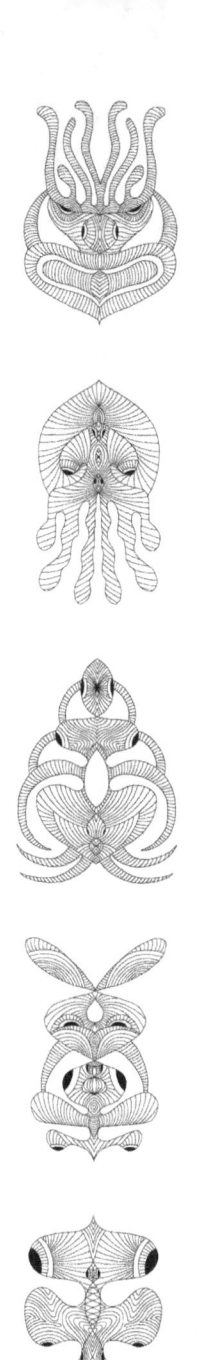
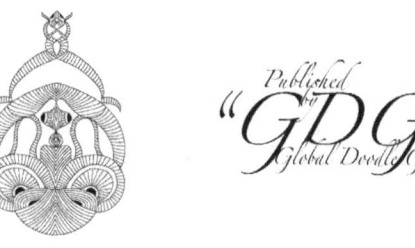
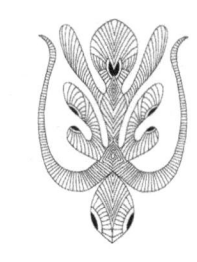

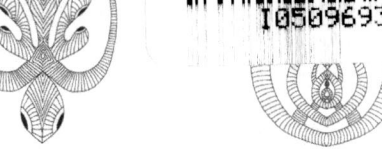
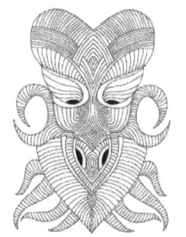
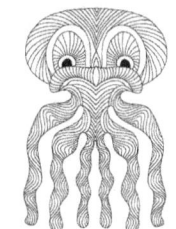

These Weirdie's belong to the collection of

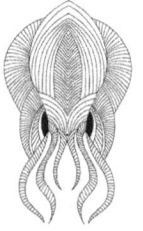
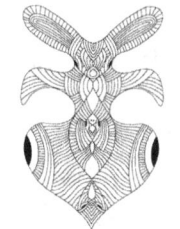
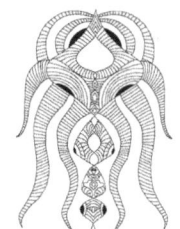
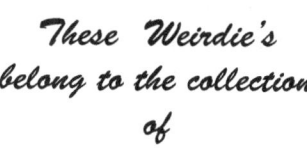
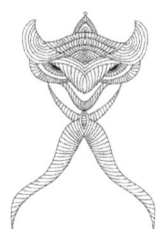
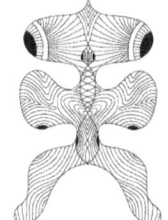
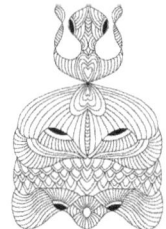
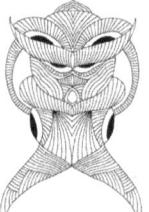
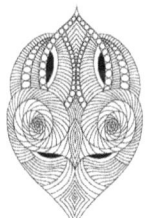
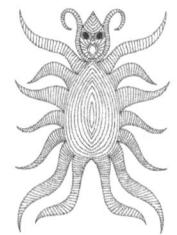
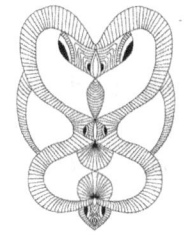
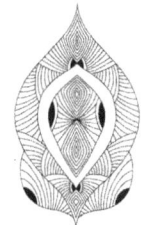
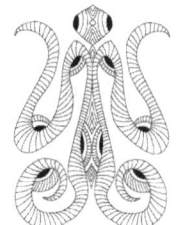
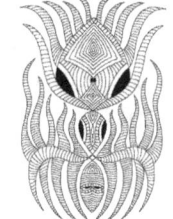
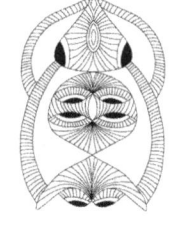
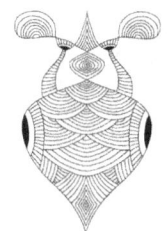
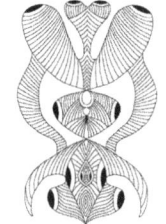
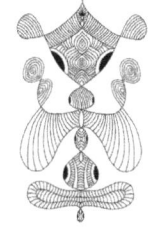
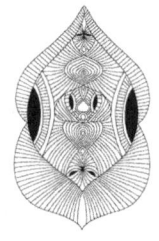
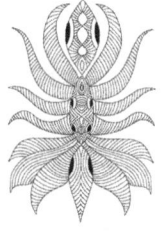

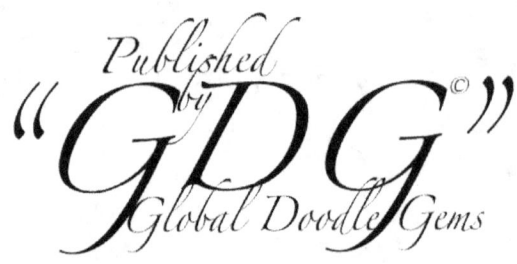

Share your colored versions with us ! We love seeing your results and hearing from you we are social !

The Official FB book page, stay on top of what we have in the works !
www.facebook.com/globaldoodlegems
The Community group, share your colored pages, meet the artists, enjoy exclusive freebies, take part in community Charity books and so much more......
www.facebook.com/groups/globaldoodlegems/
Follow us on Twitter.... @GlobalDoodlegem
We are on Instagram too
@globaldoodlegems for instagram
...and if you are not social like that we have a blog
globaldoodlegems.wordpress.com

Copyright © 2016 Global Doodle Gems
All rights are reserved by Global Doodle Gems.
Duplication of pages for personal use are allowed. You are invited to color the pages then scan/post your coloured versions to social networks, mentioning the book title and author/artist (Global Doodle Gems).
All artwork and images are protected by copyright laws. This book or any portion thereof may not, otherwise, be reproduced and/or distributed or transmitted without the express written permission of the artist/publisher of Global Doodle Gems.
All of us from the Global Doodle Gems wish you a colortastic time and look forward to seeing your wonderful color results online !

Welcome to my world of Weirdies

This series of drawings are dedicated to all the weird, whimsical,
wacky and totally amazing people in the world !
The Weirdie's is a Weirdie a day Challenge !
Hopefully they will put a smile on your face,
and hours of fun to color...
There will be 12 books, one for each month of the year, with
a Weirdie for each day.... some of the Weirdies can also
be colored upside down... in the books I will include
upside down extras of those Weirdies that may apply...
This is the ninth of the 12 books...
and is the book of September weirdies...
follow me on my artpage facebook AMVWART
I will try to post my colored daily ...
and keep you updated on new releases.
Please feel free to share yours with me ...
I would love to see them...
I hope you will enjoy my Weirdie World !
Sending out a huge embrace to all of you !

Maria Wedel

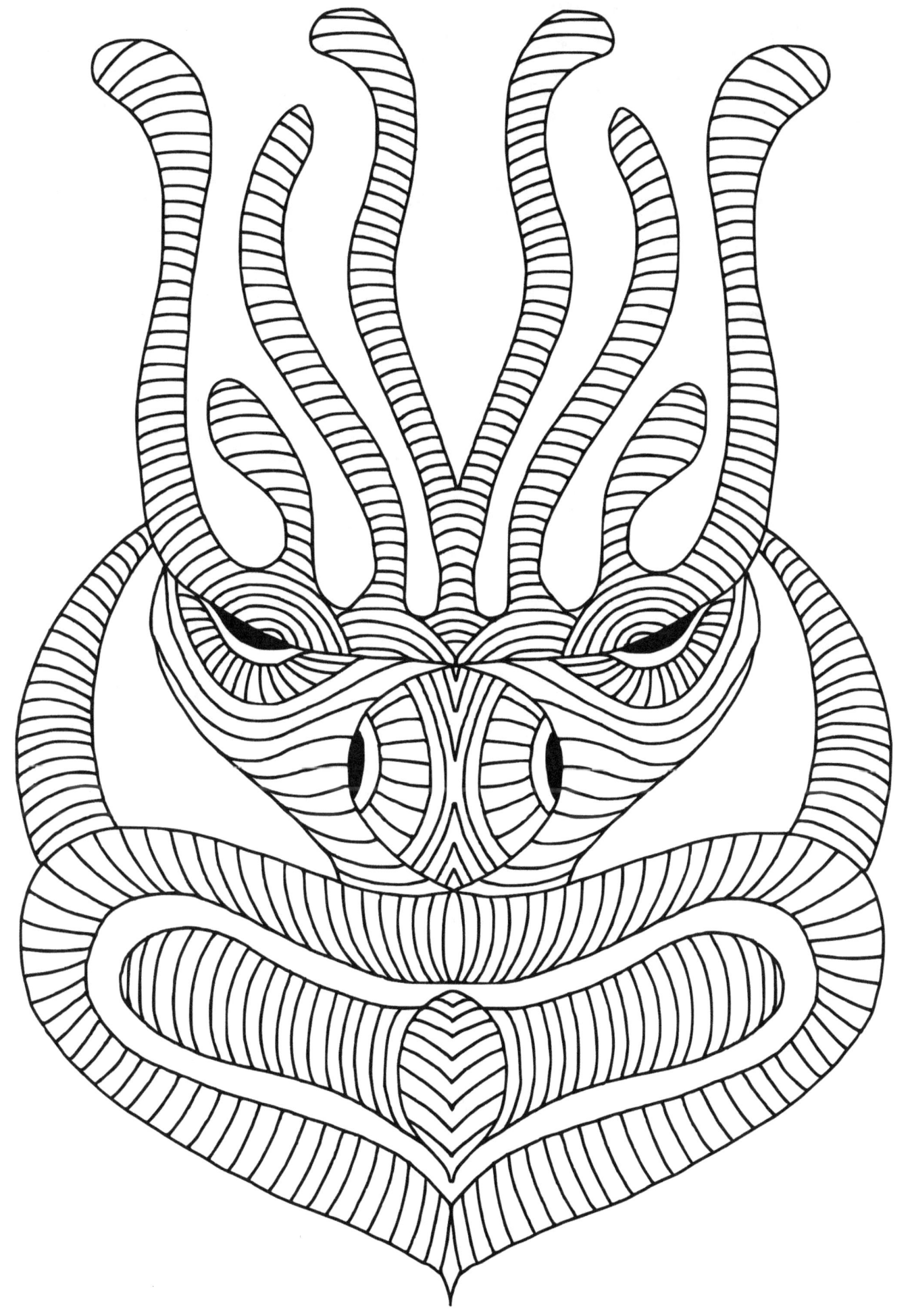

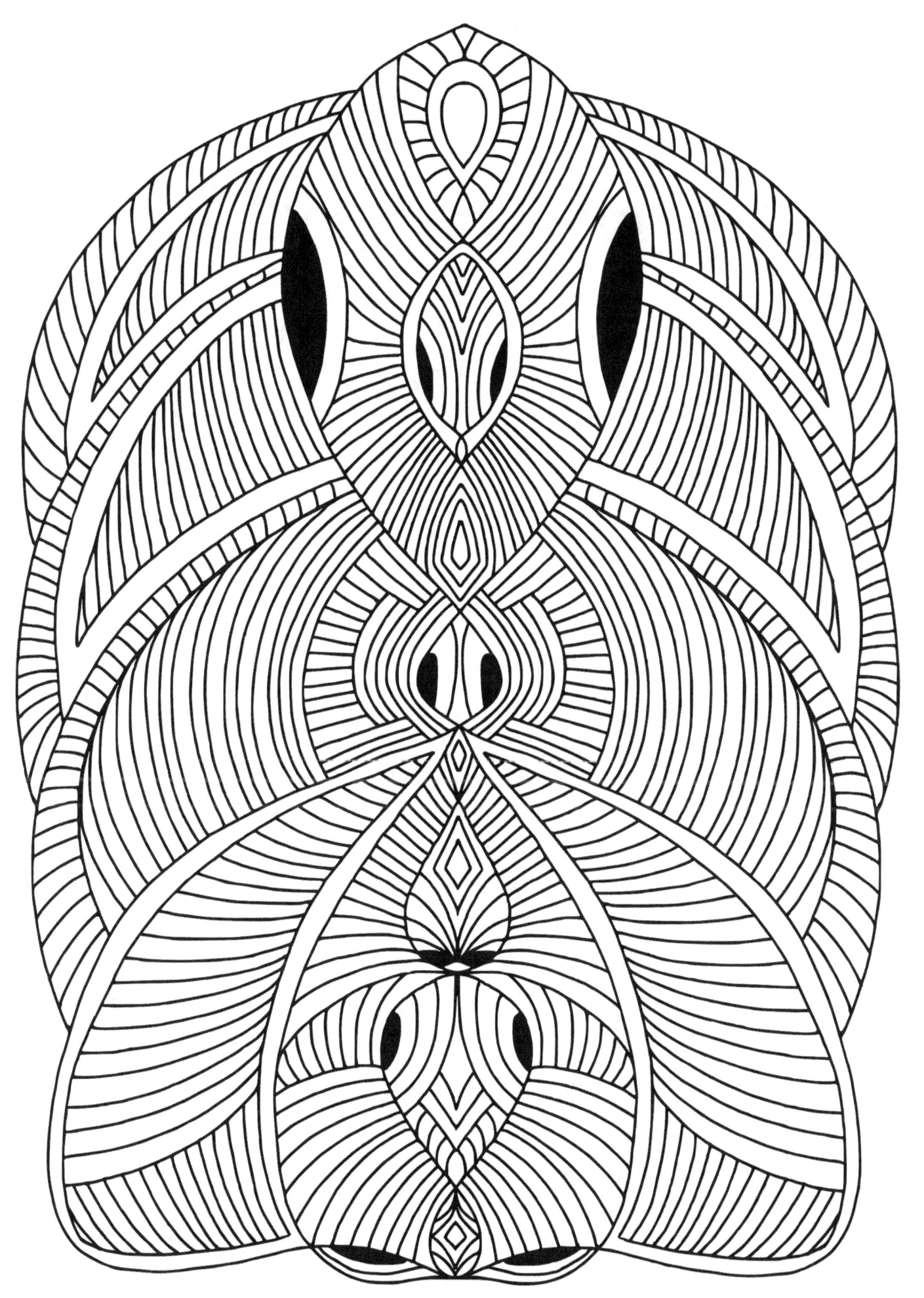

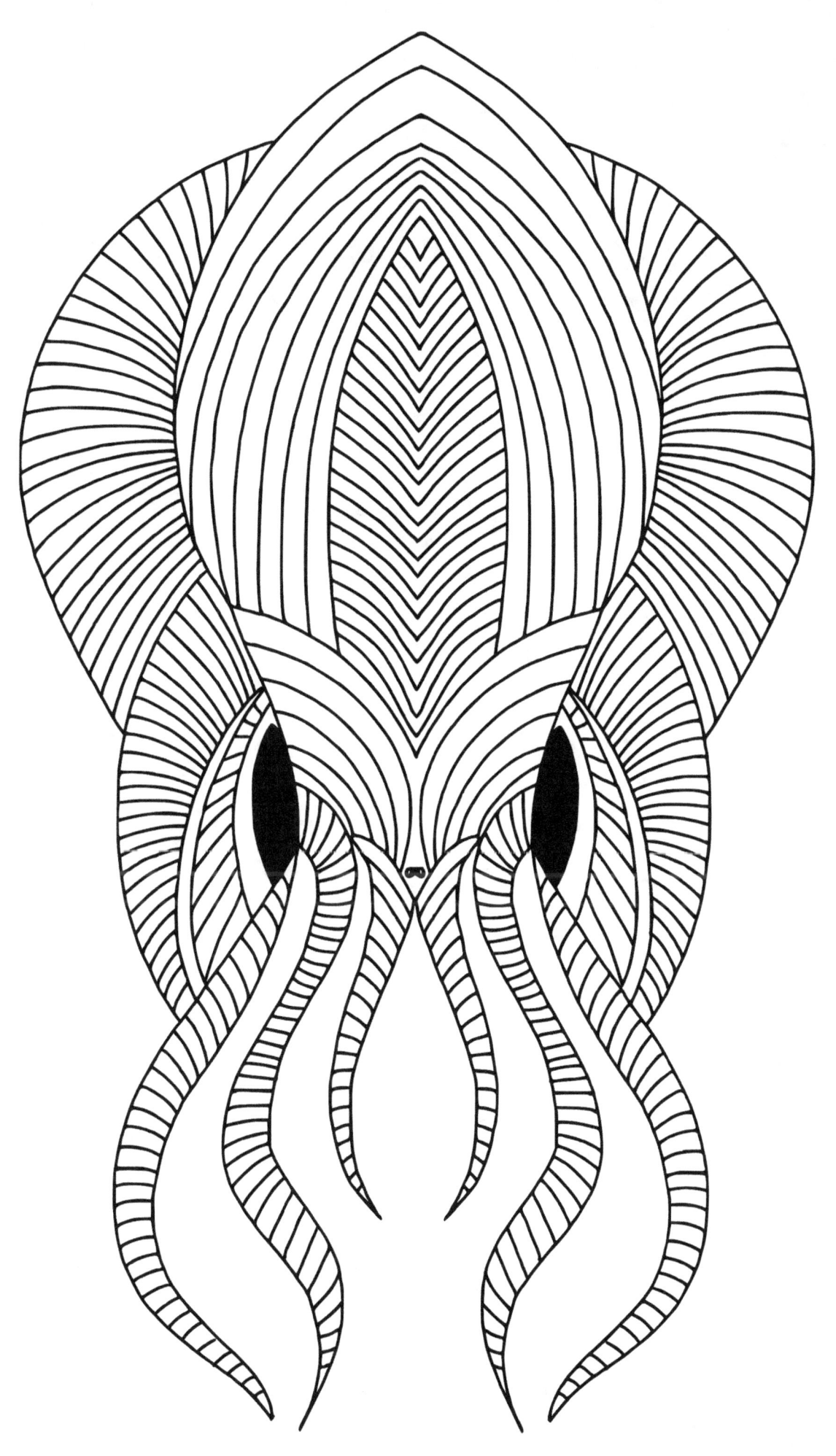

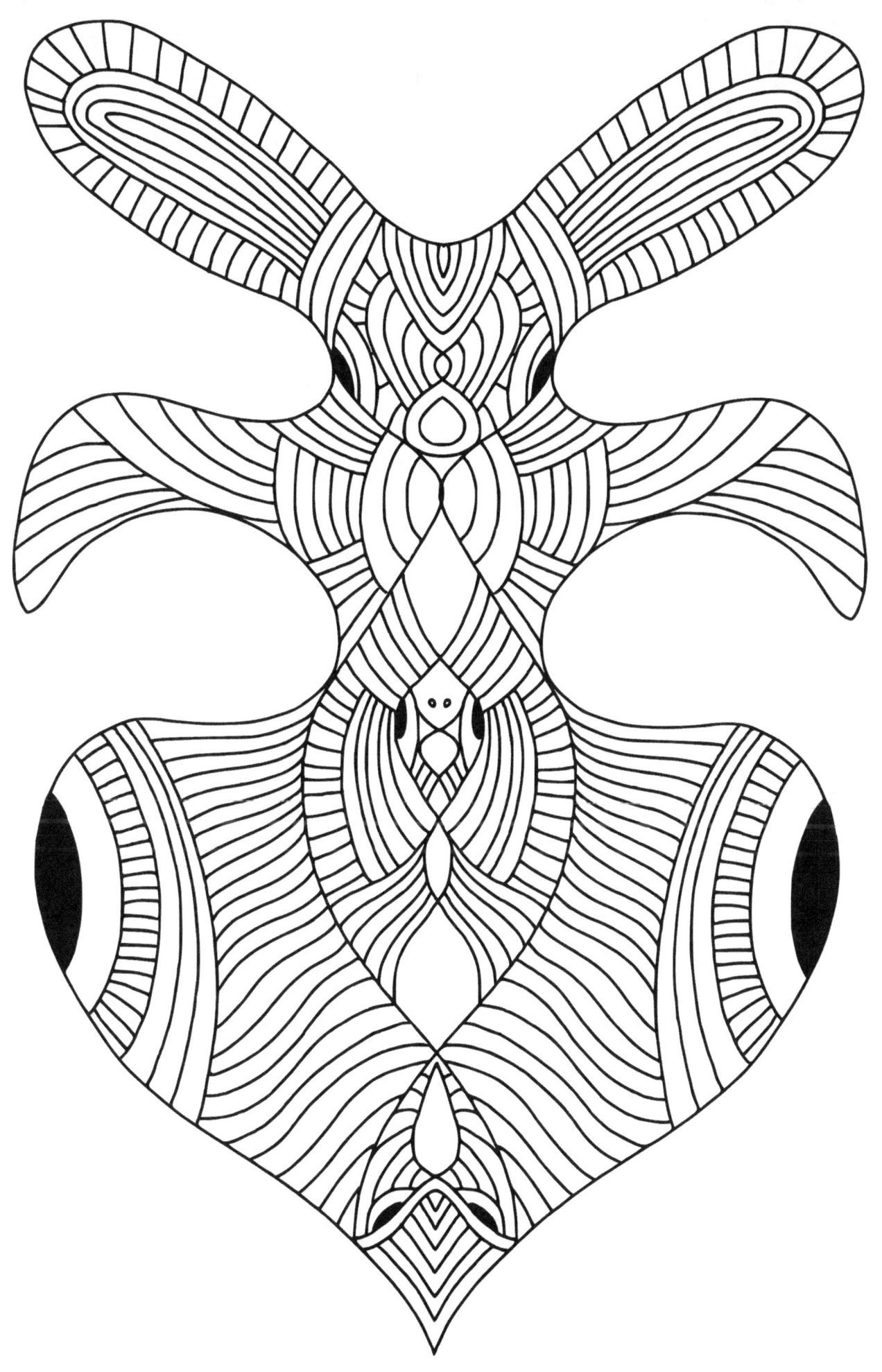

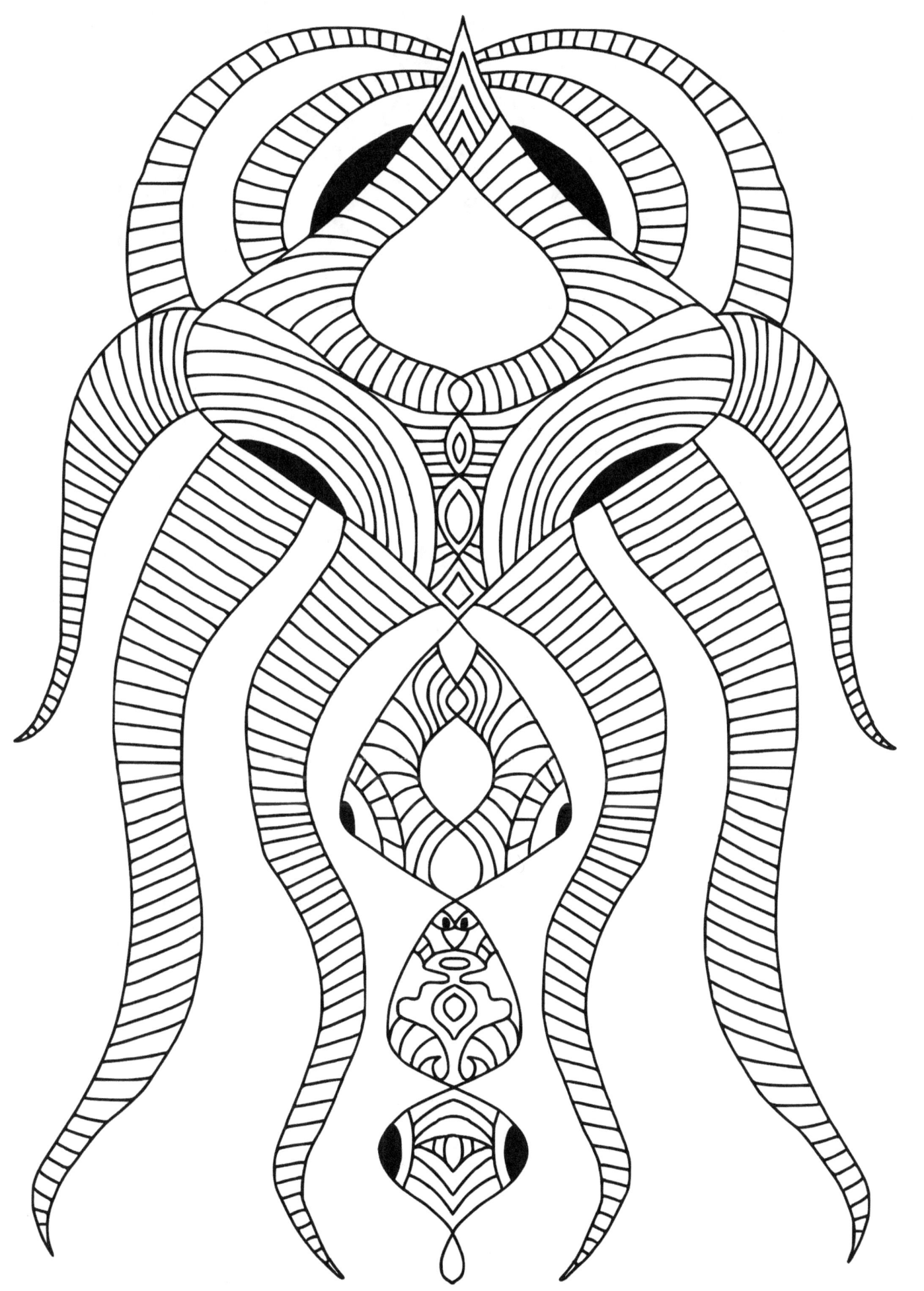

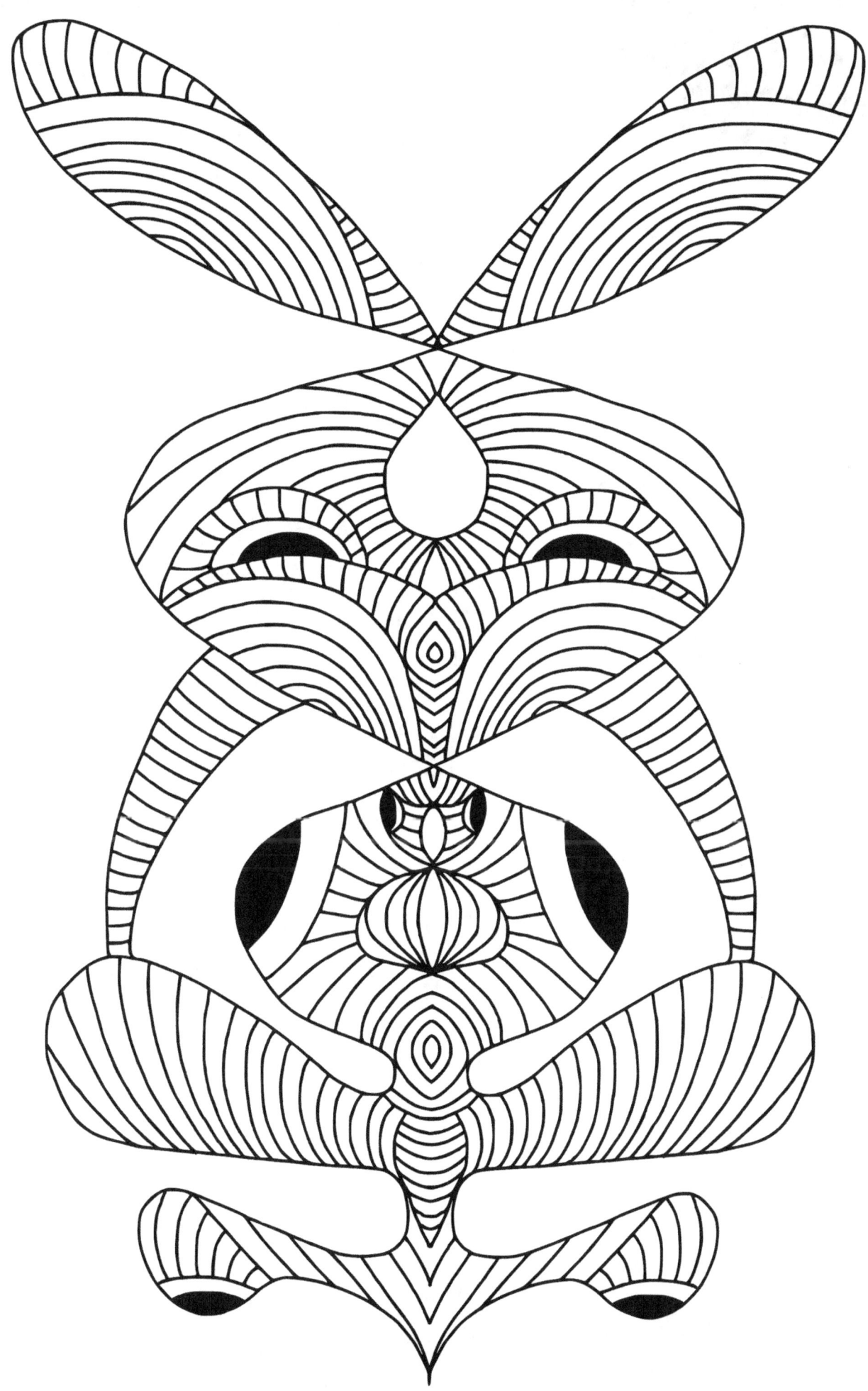

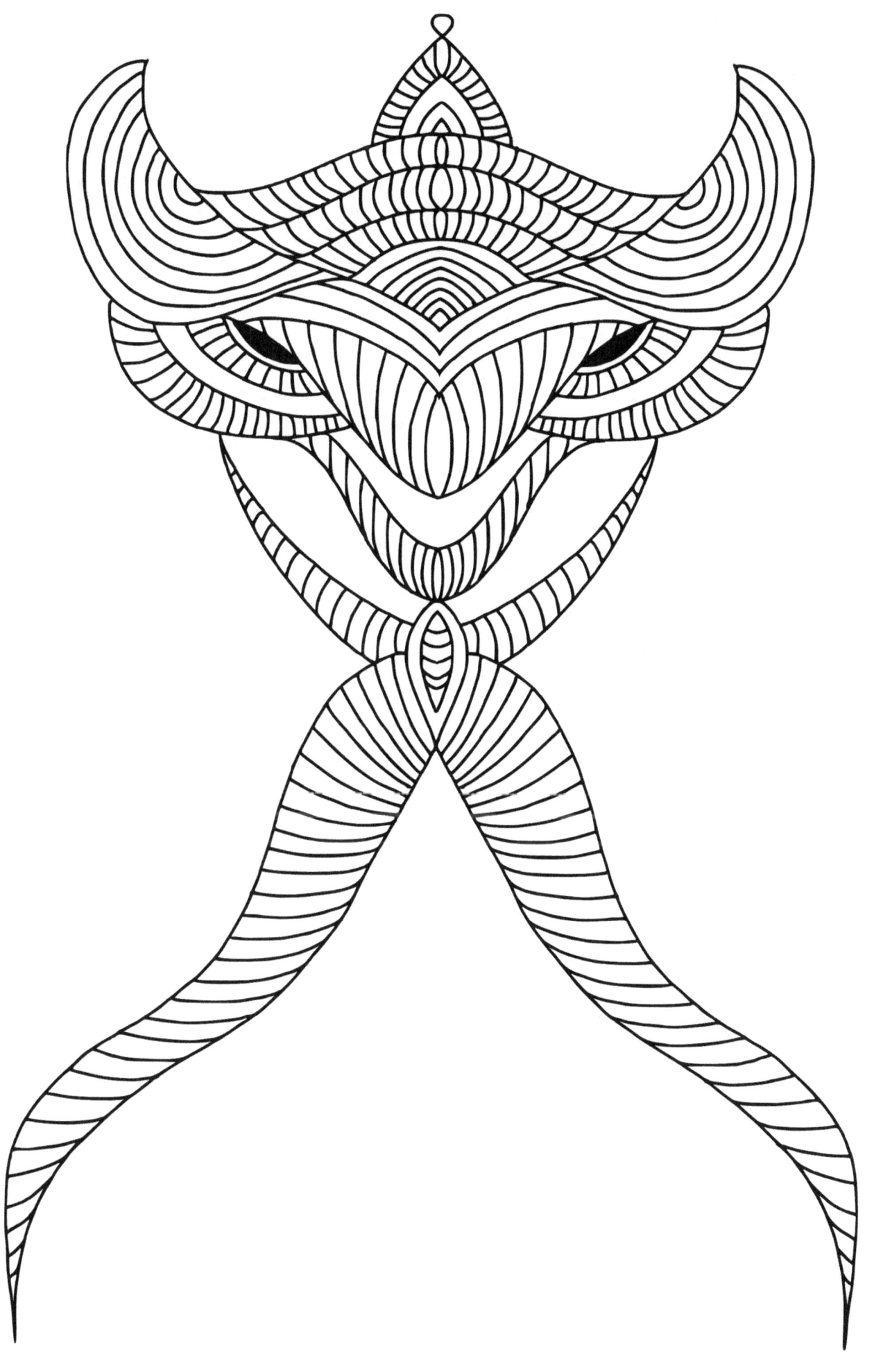

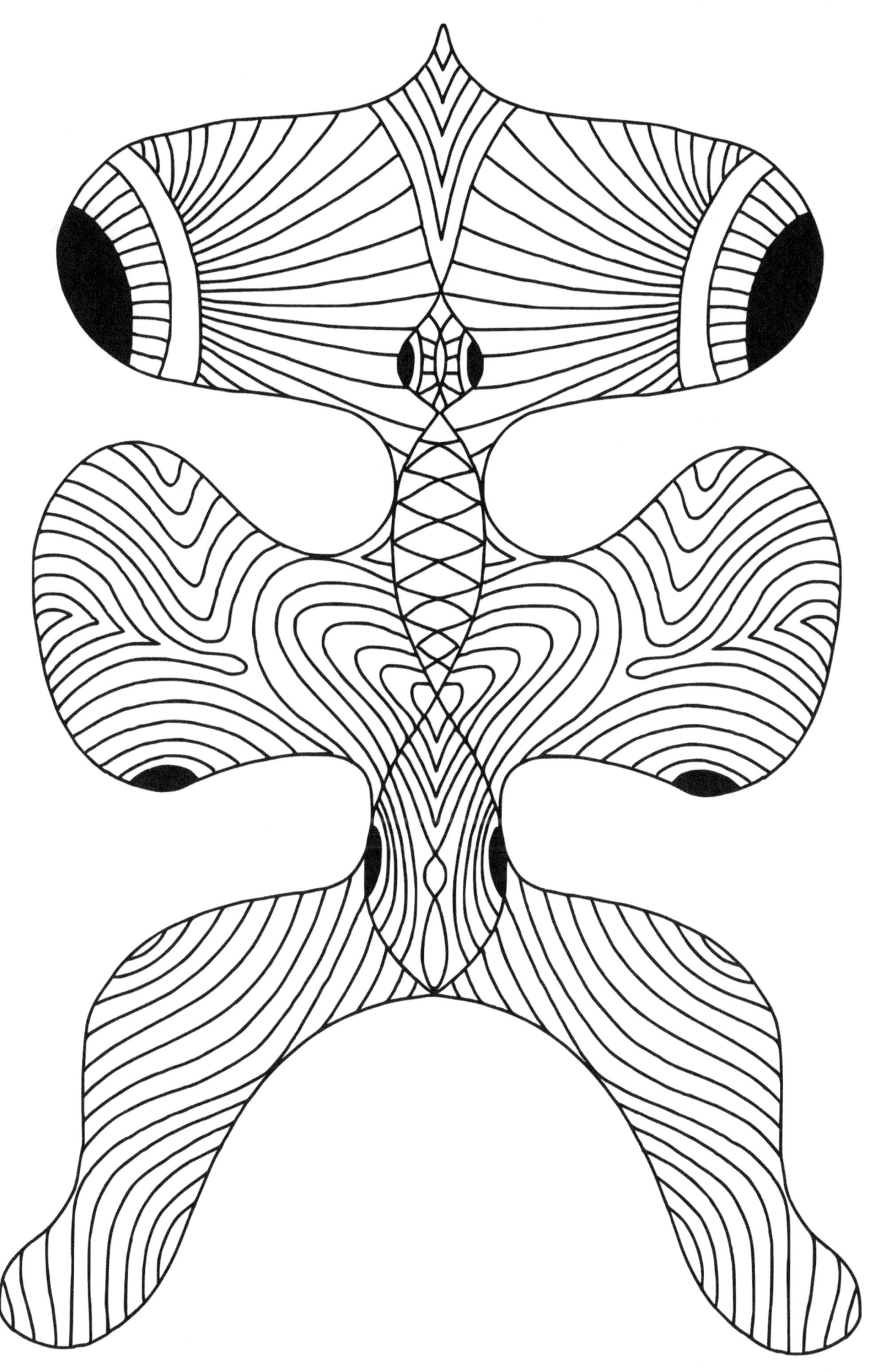

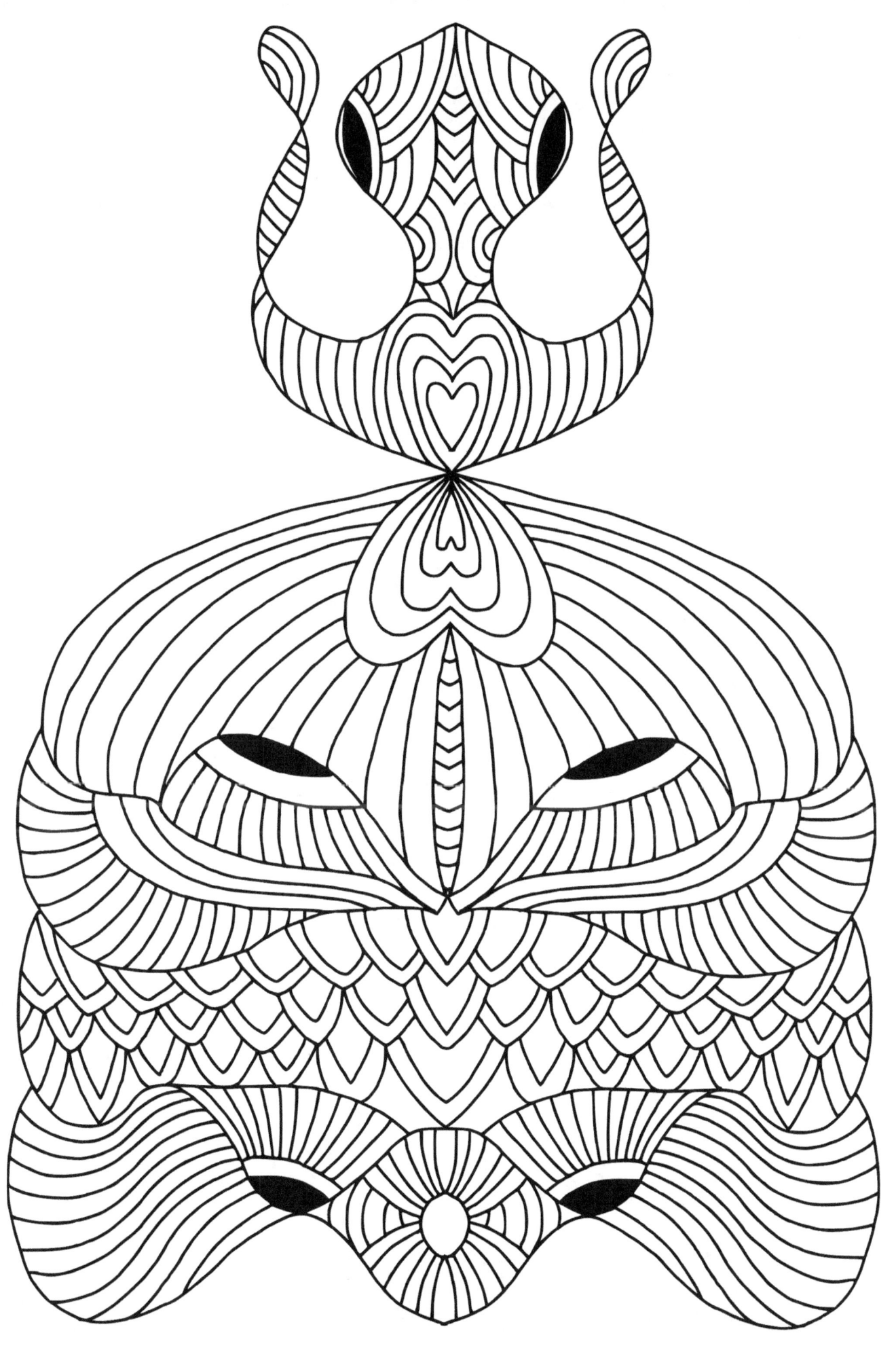

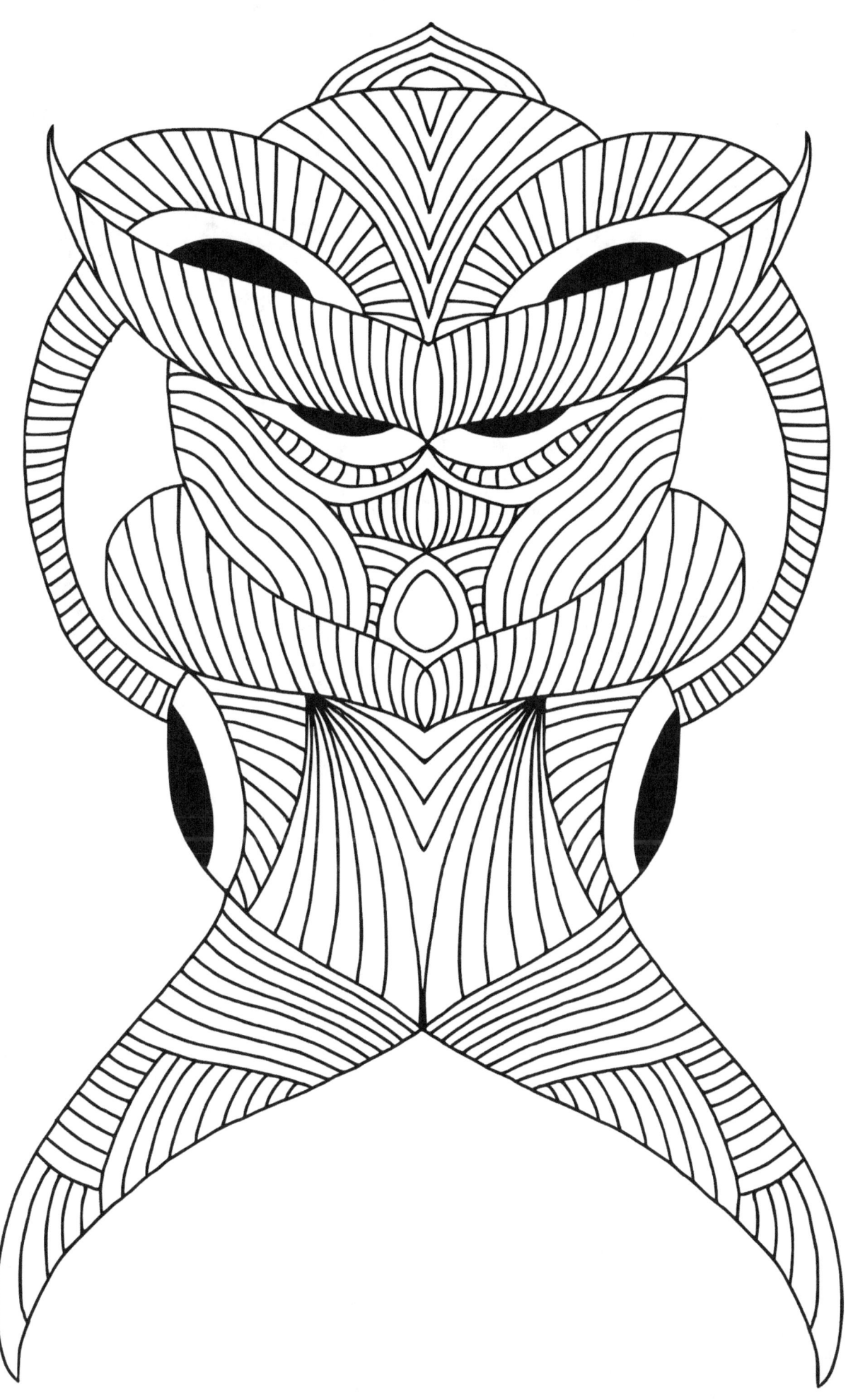

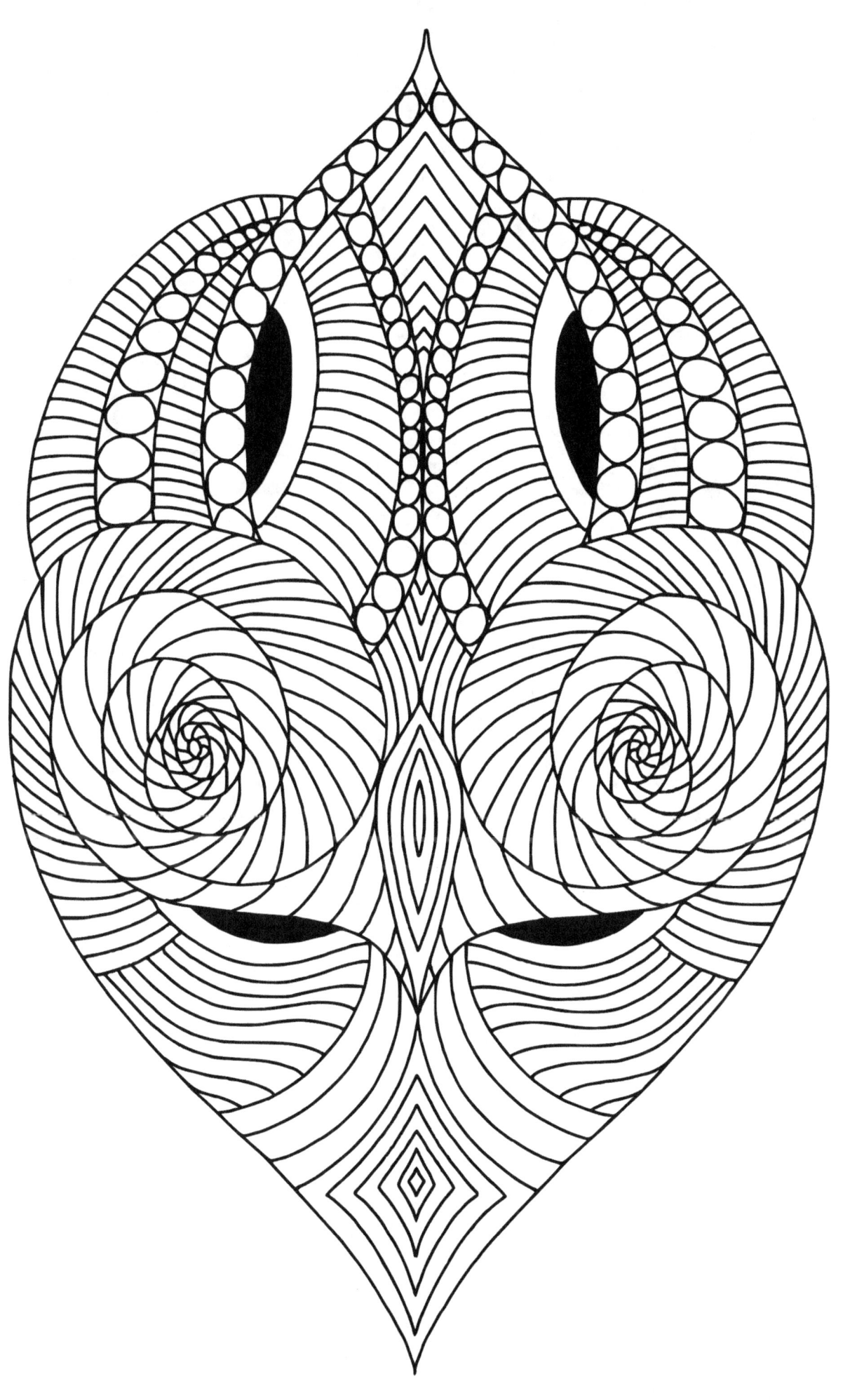

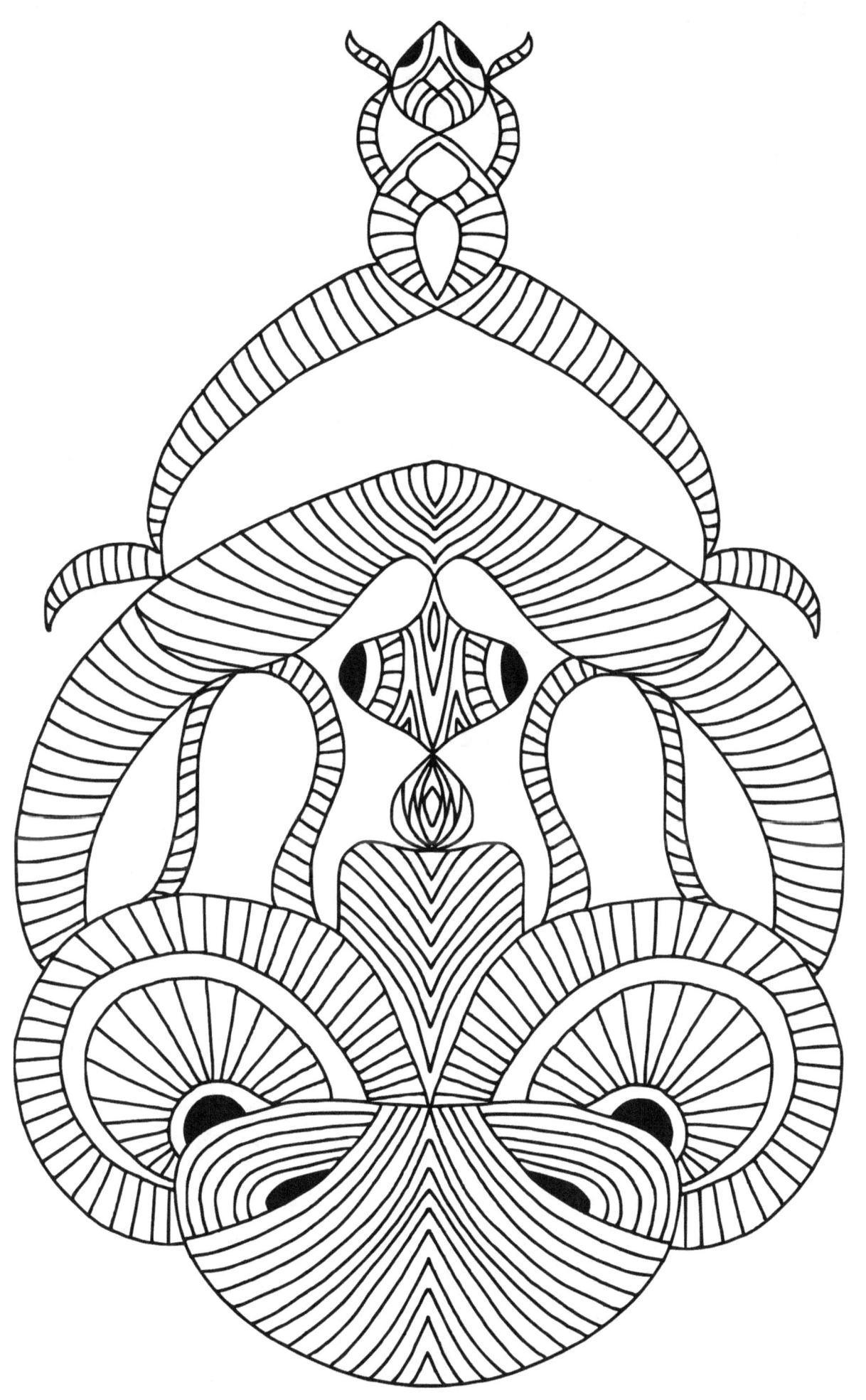

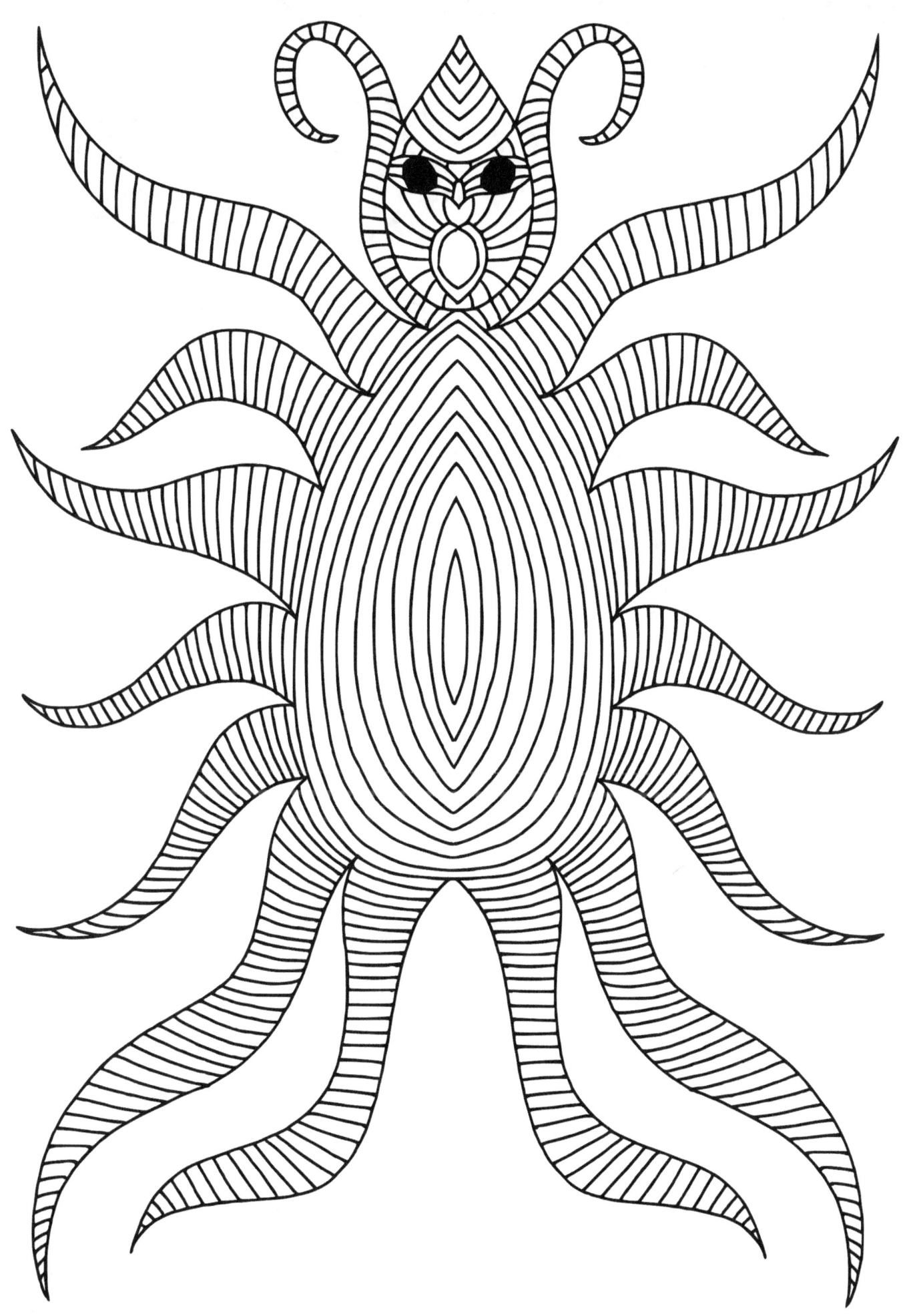

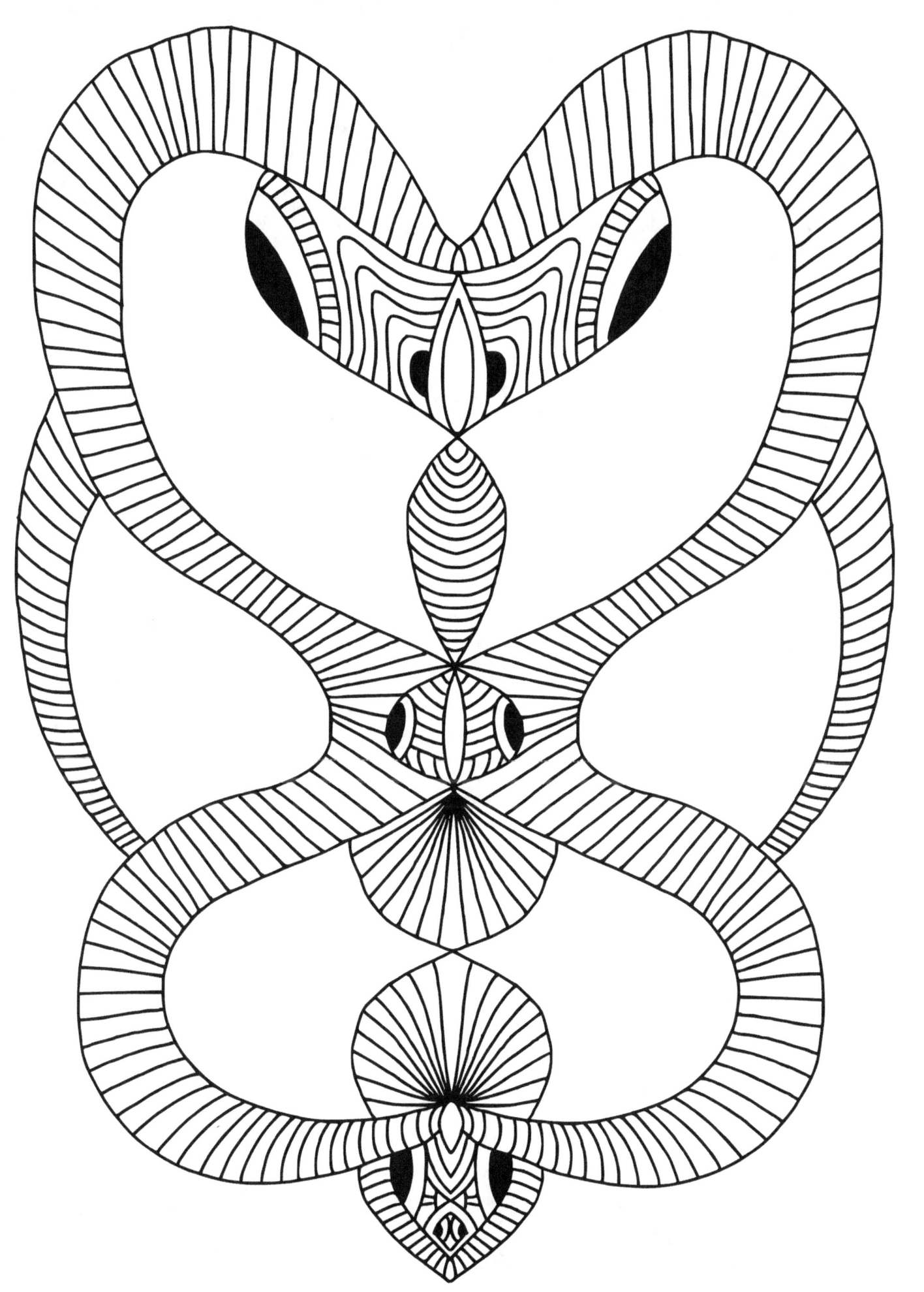

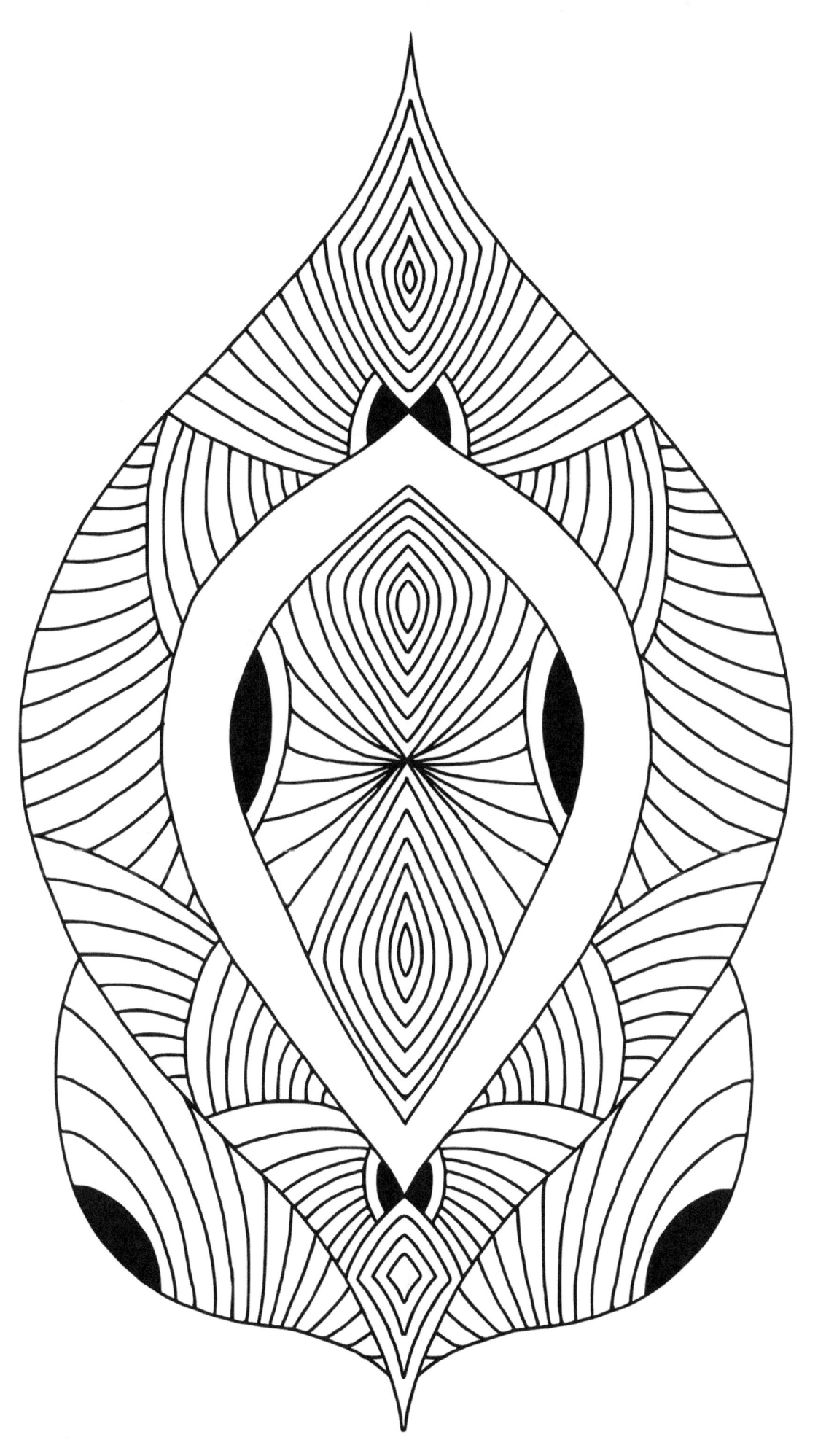

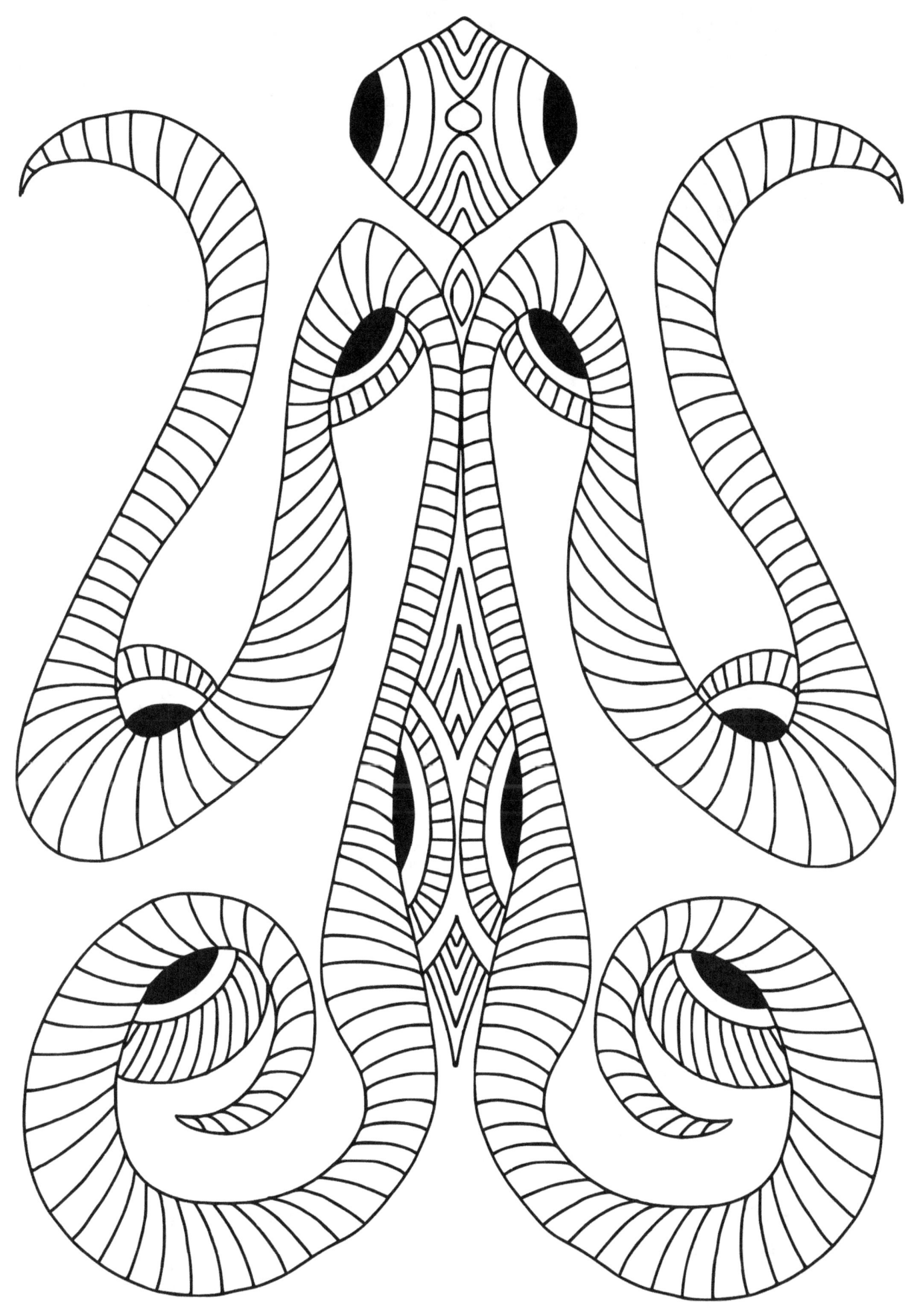

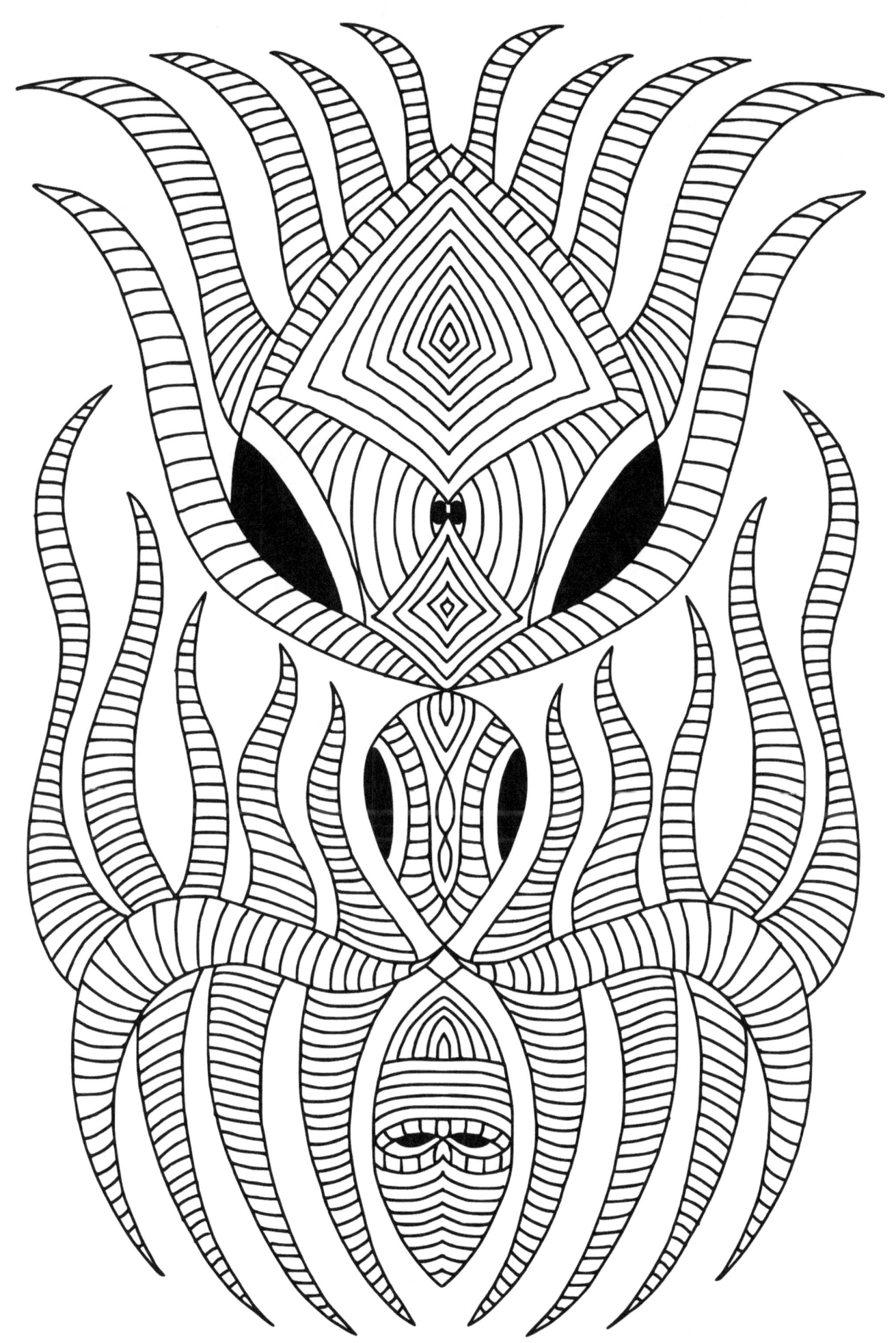

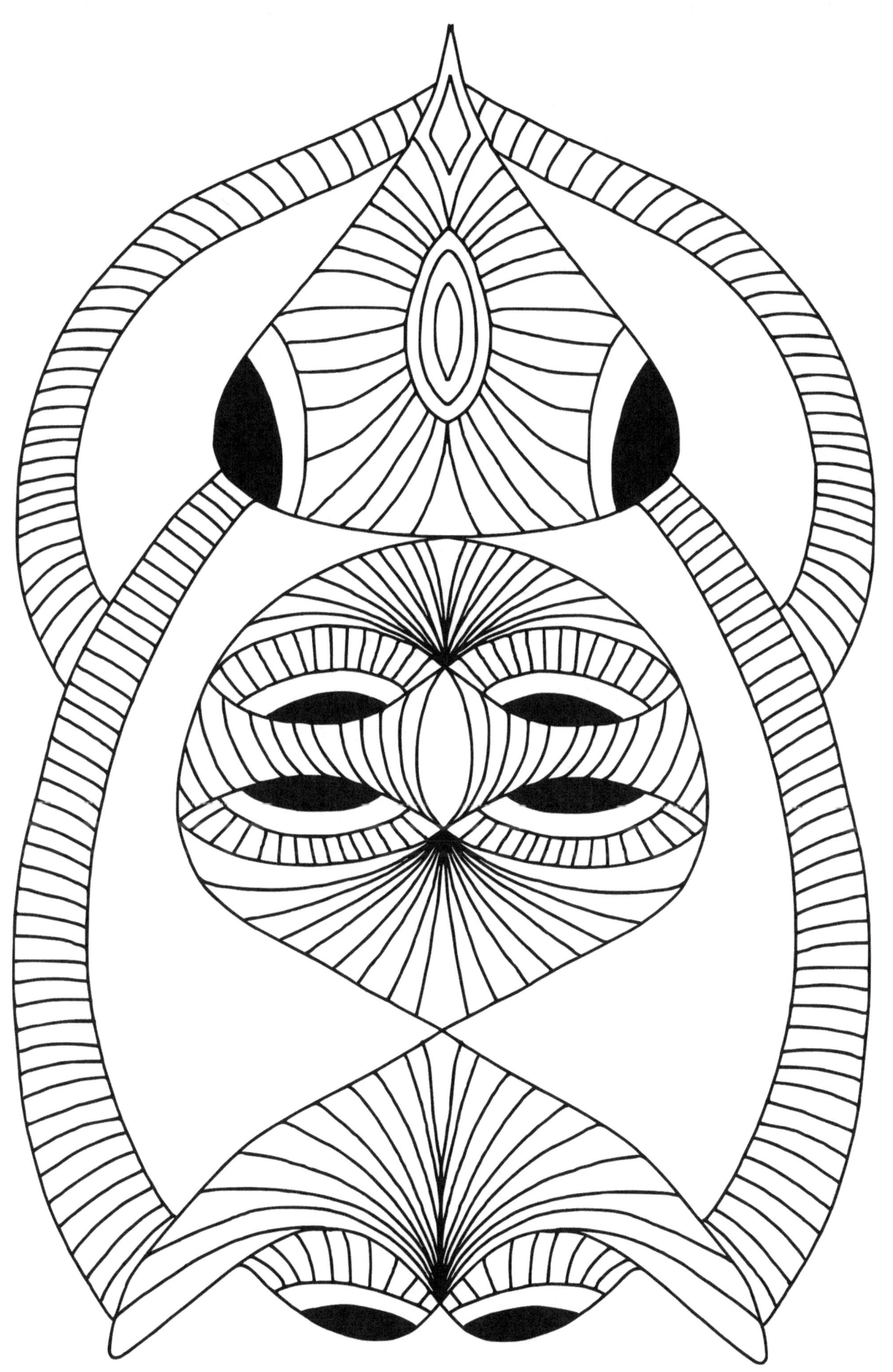

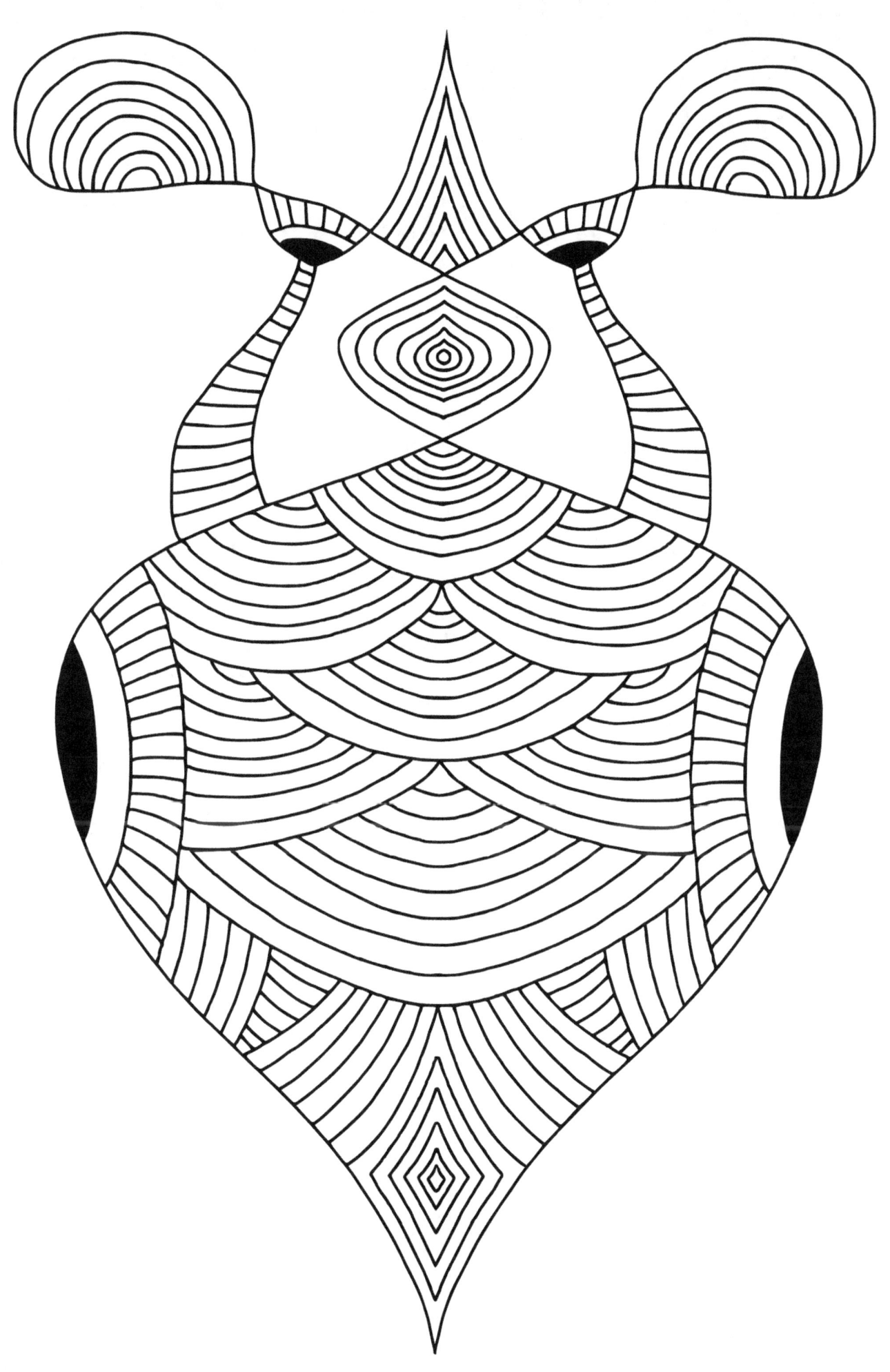

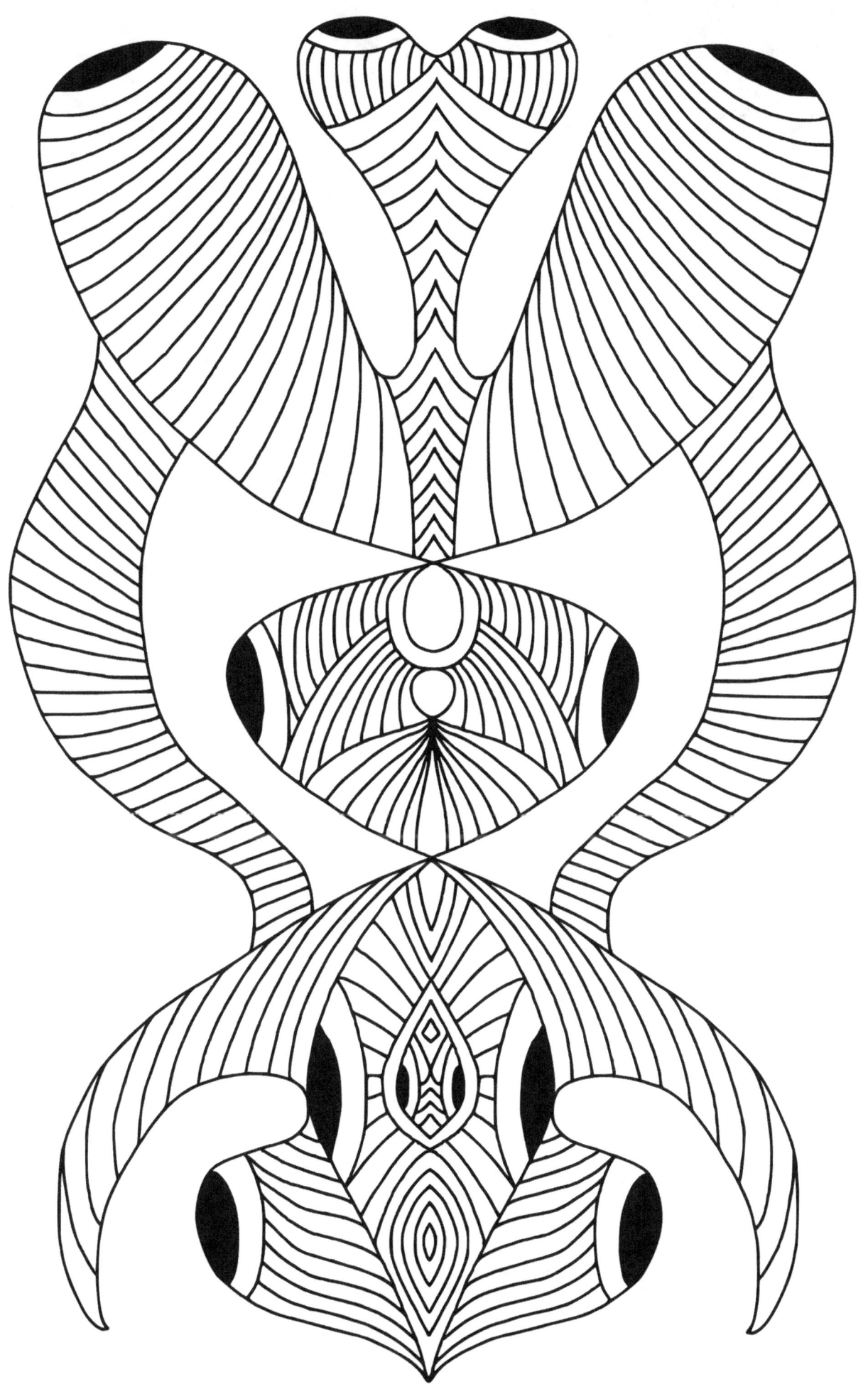

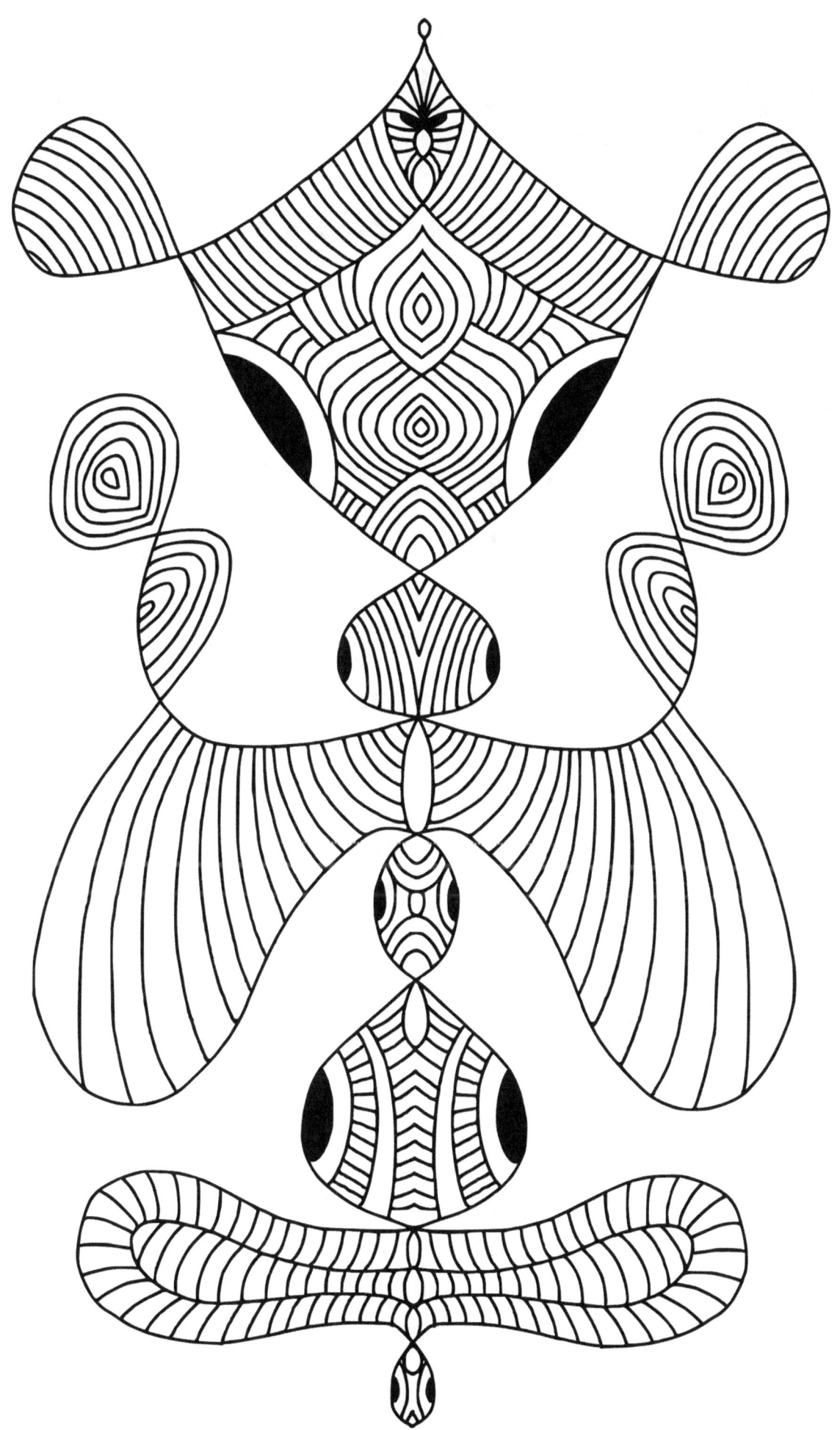

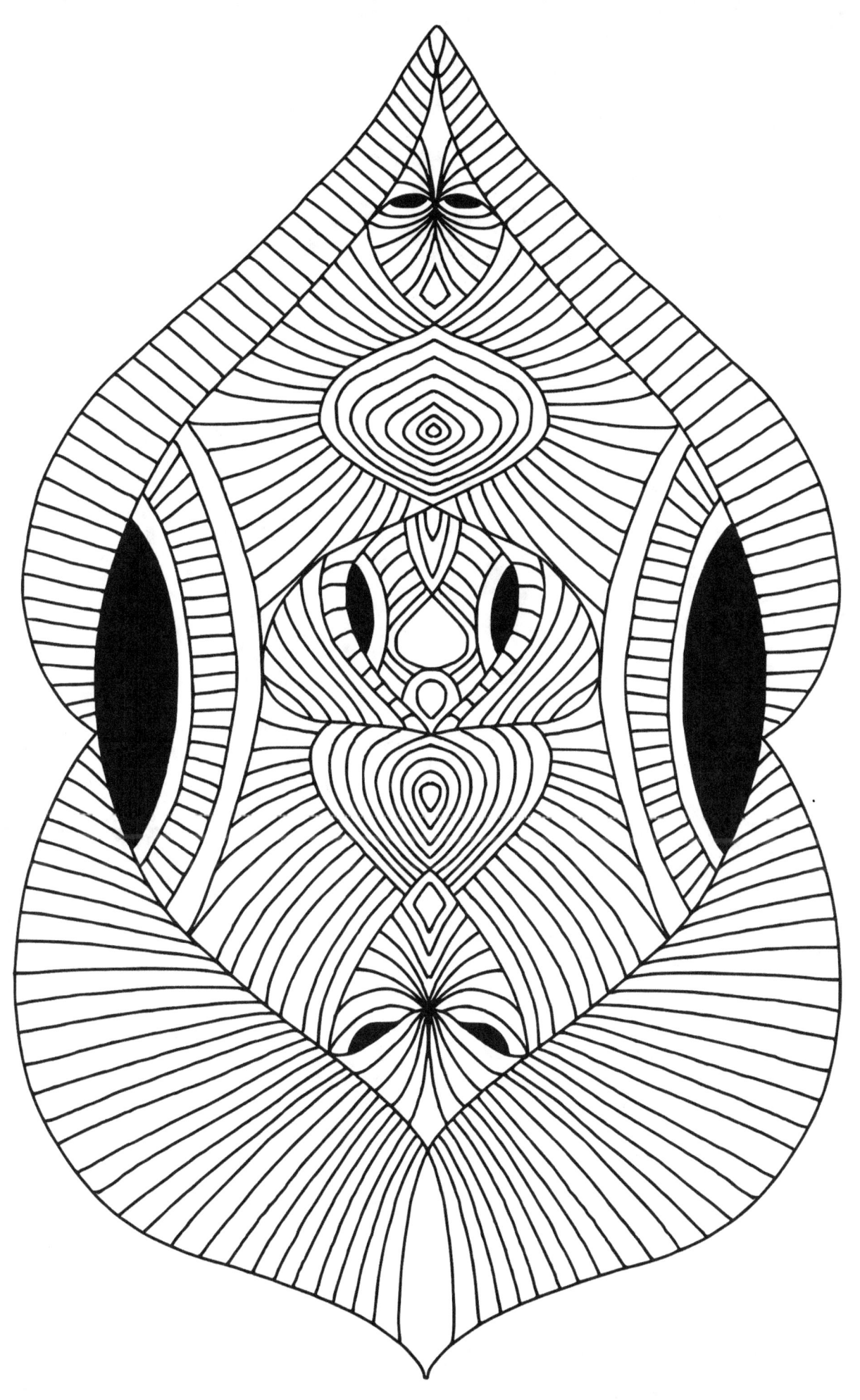

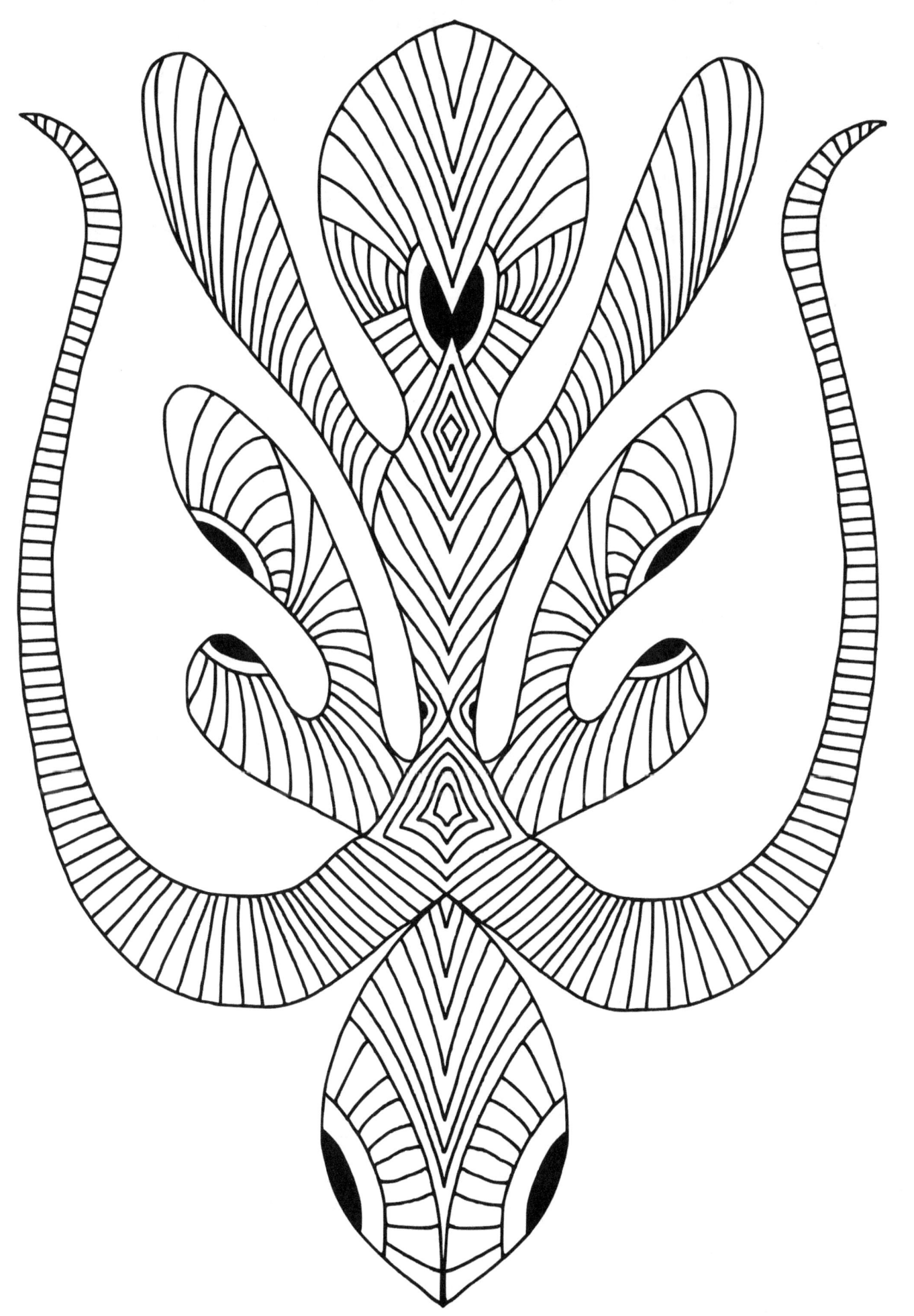

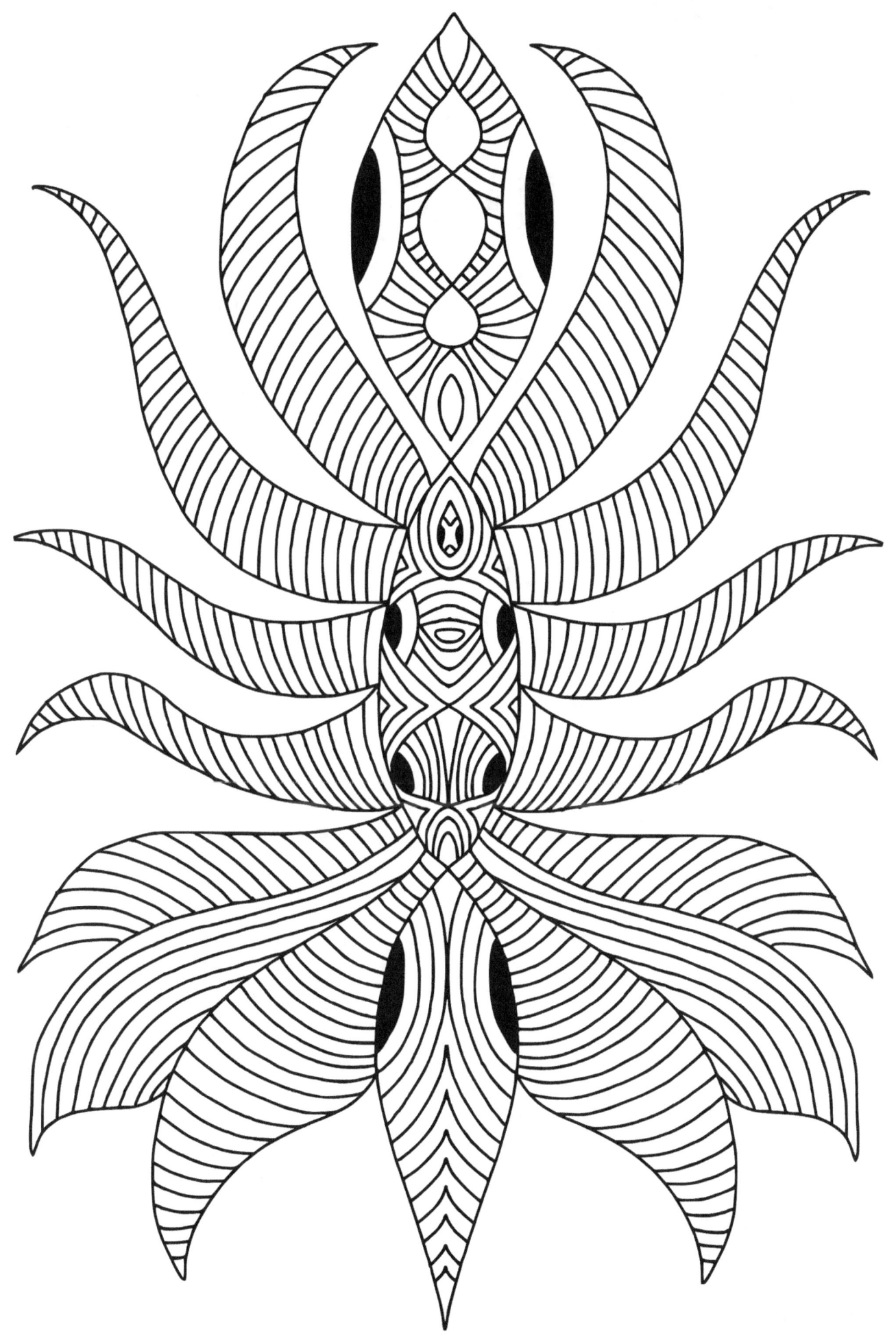

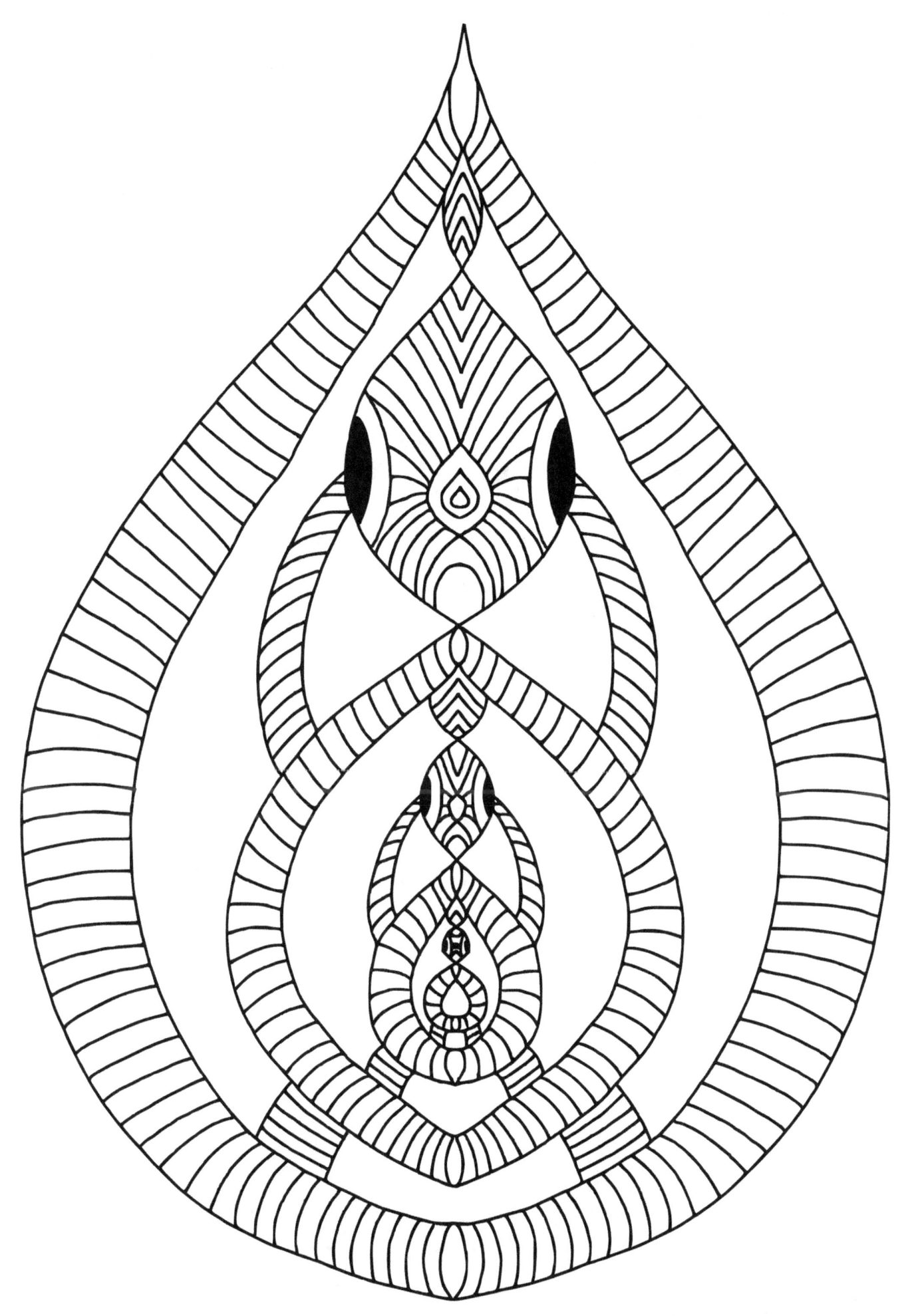

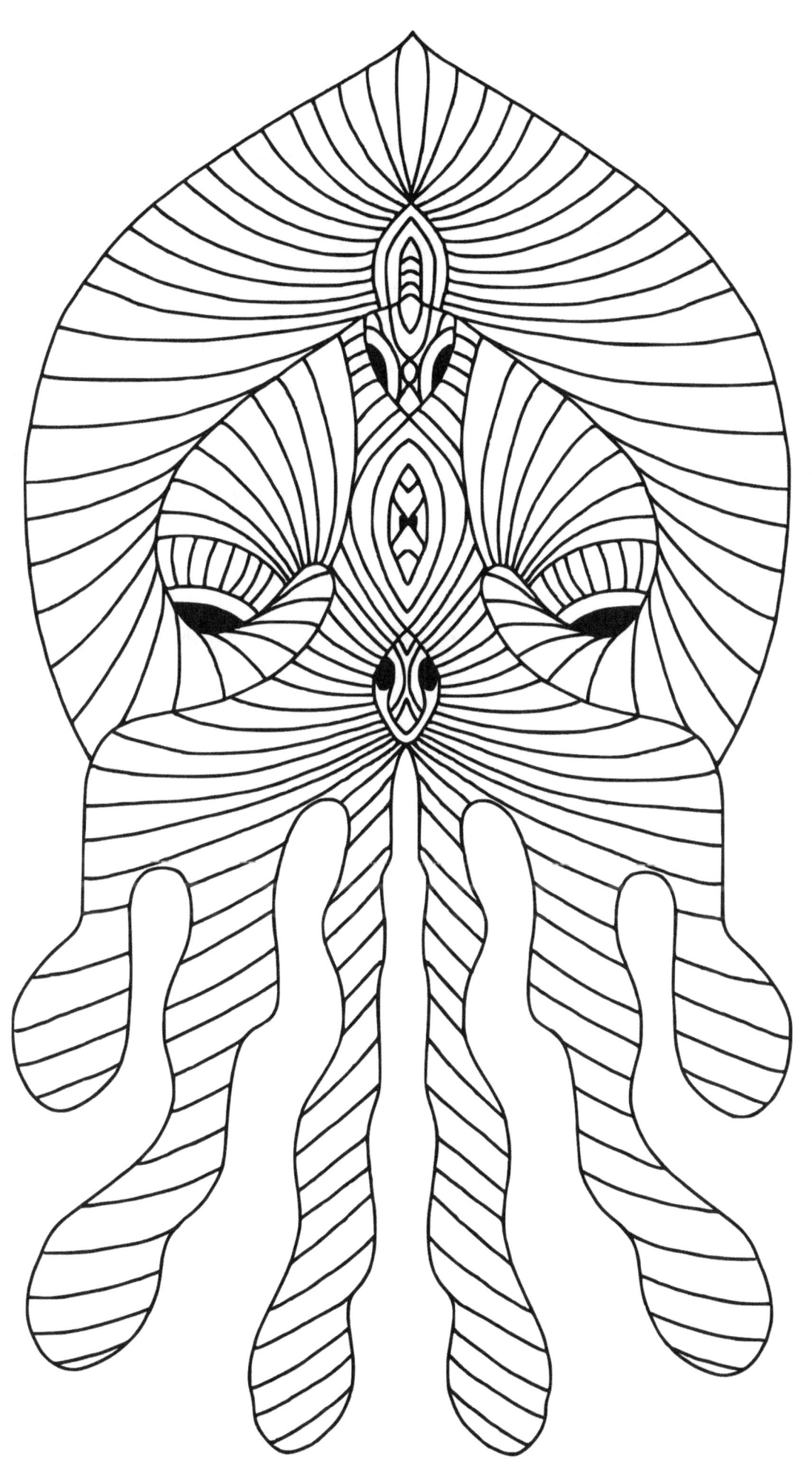

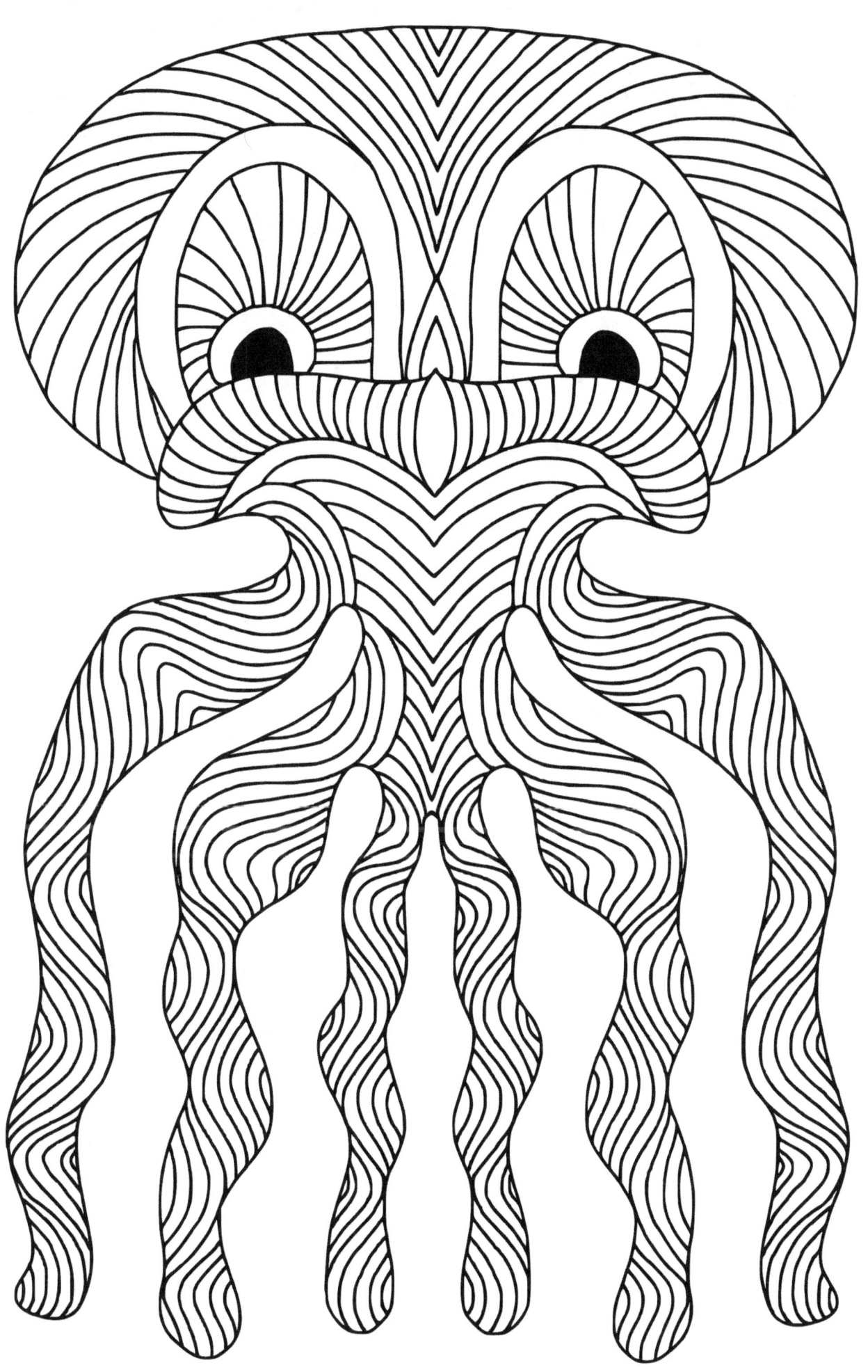

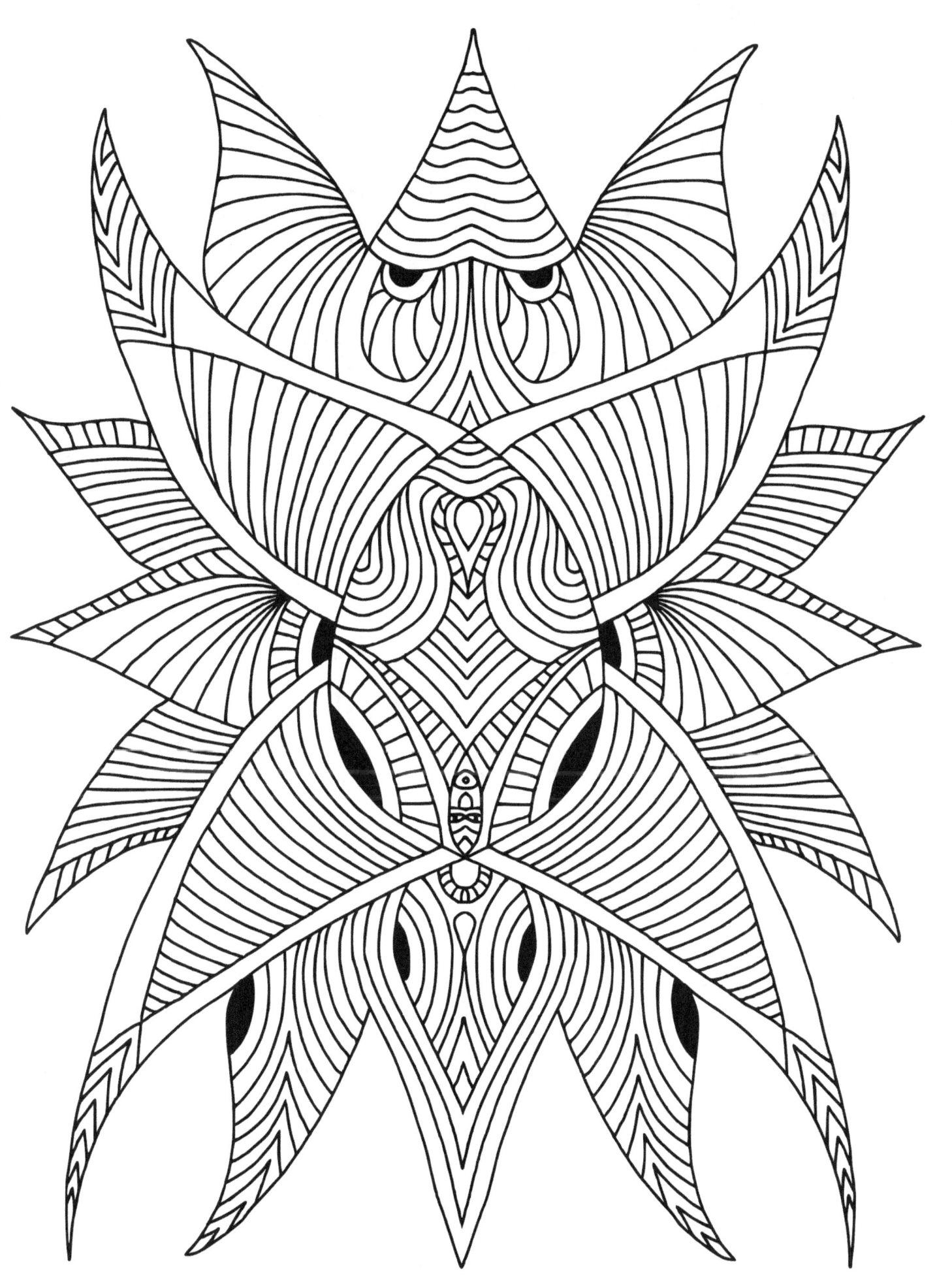

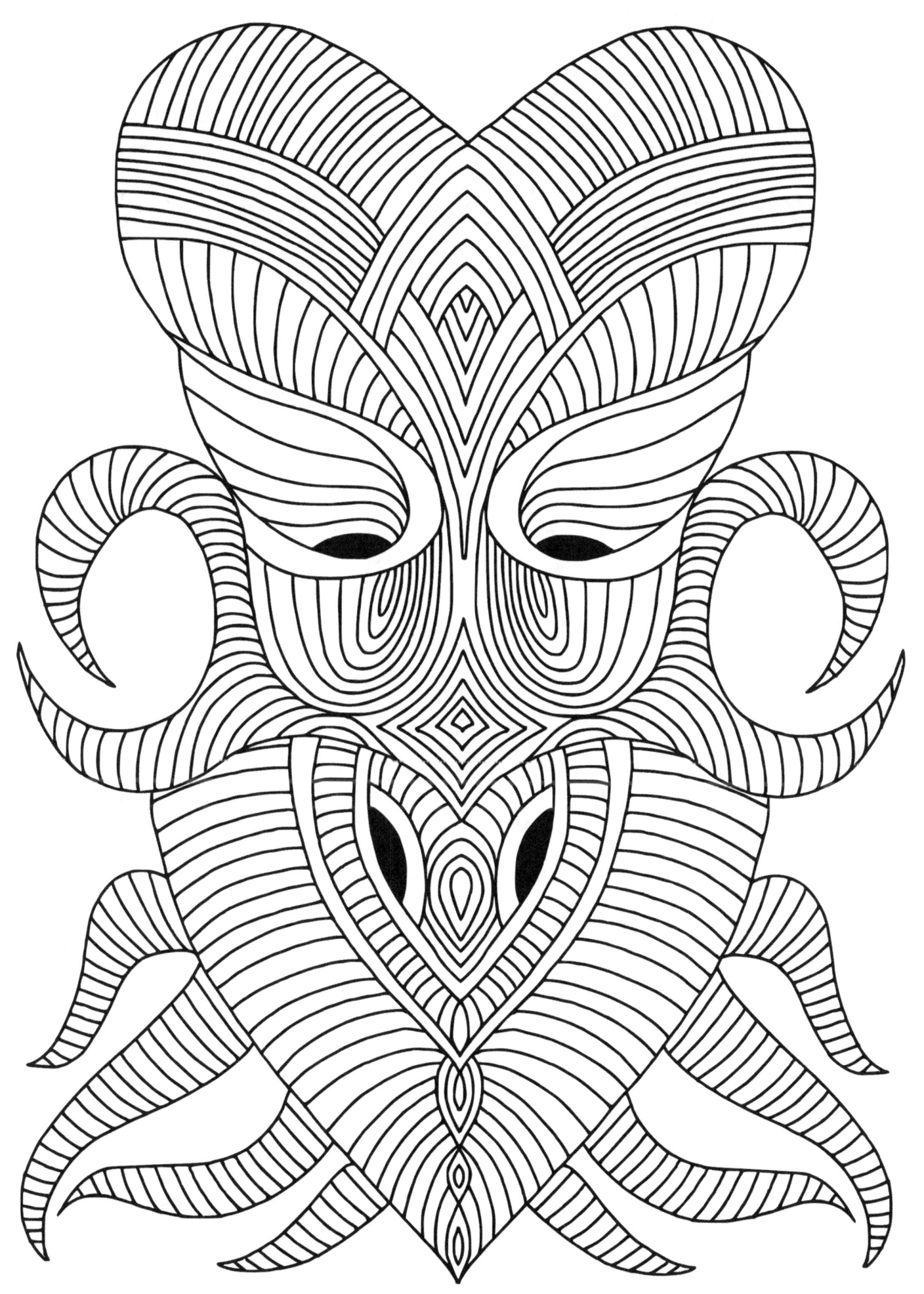

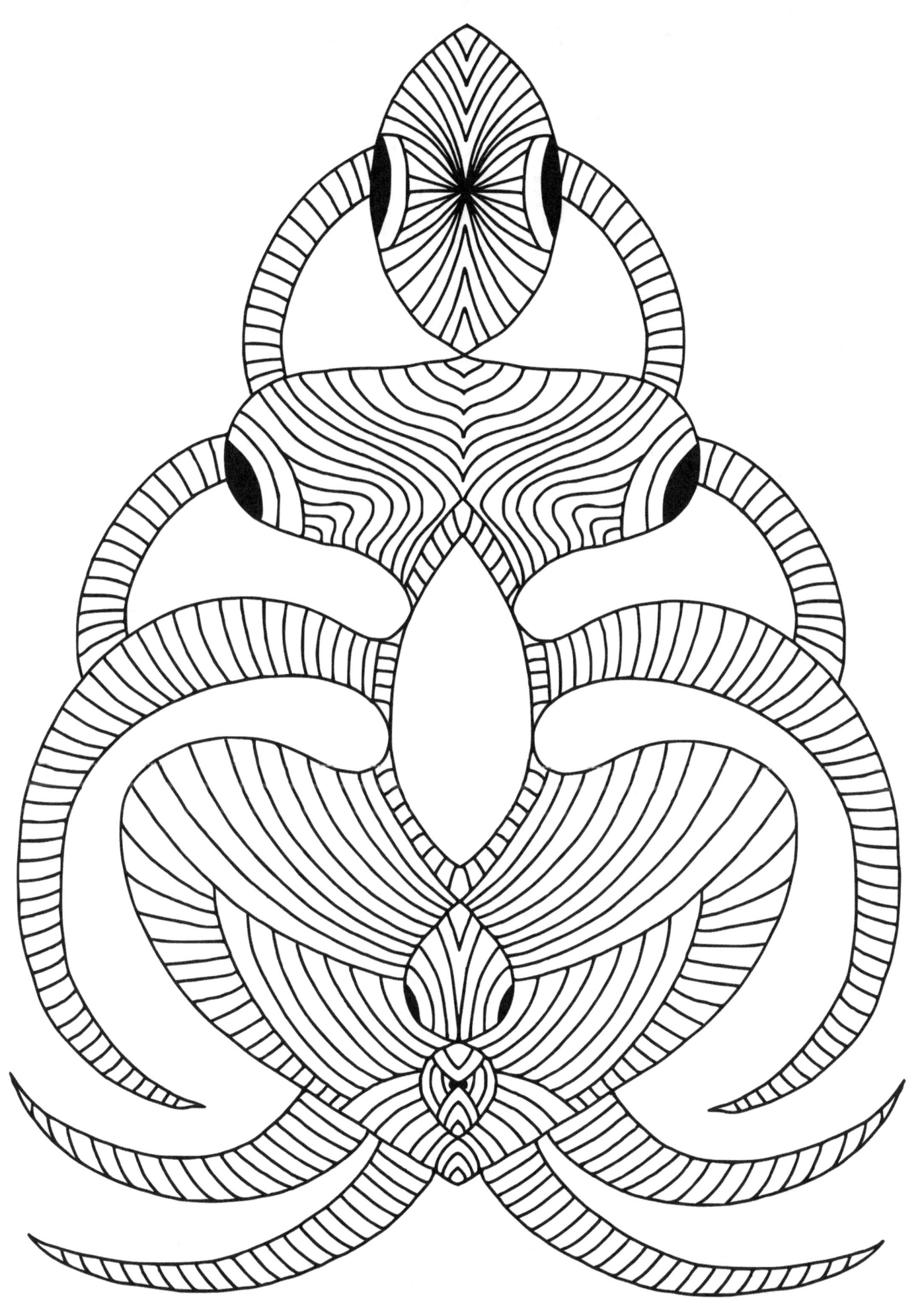

Bonus 30 Upside Down versions......

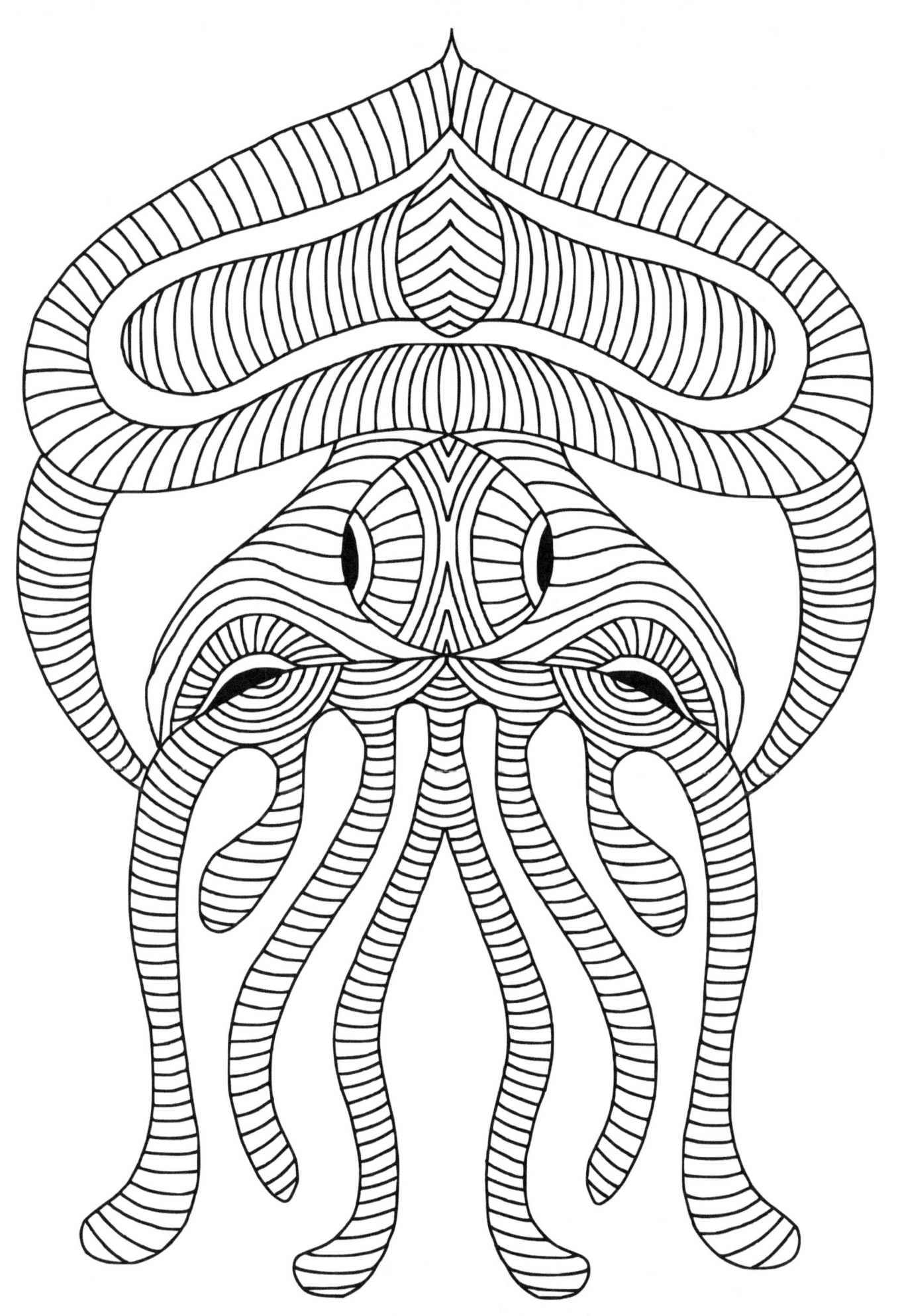

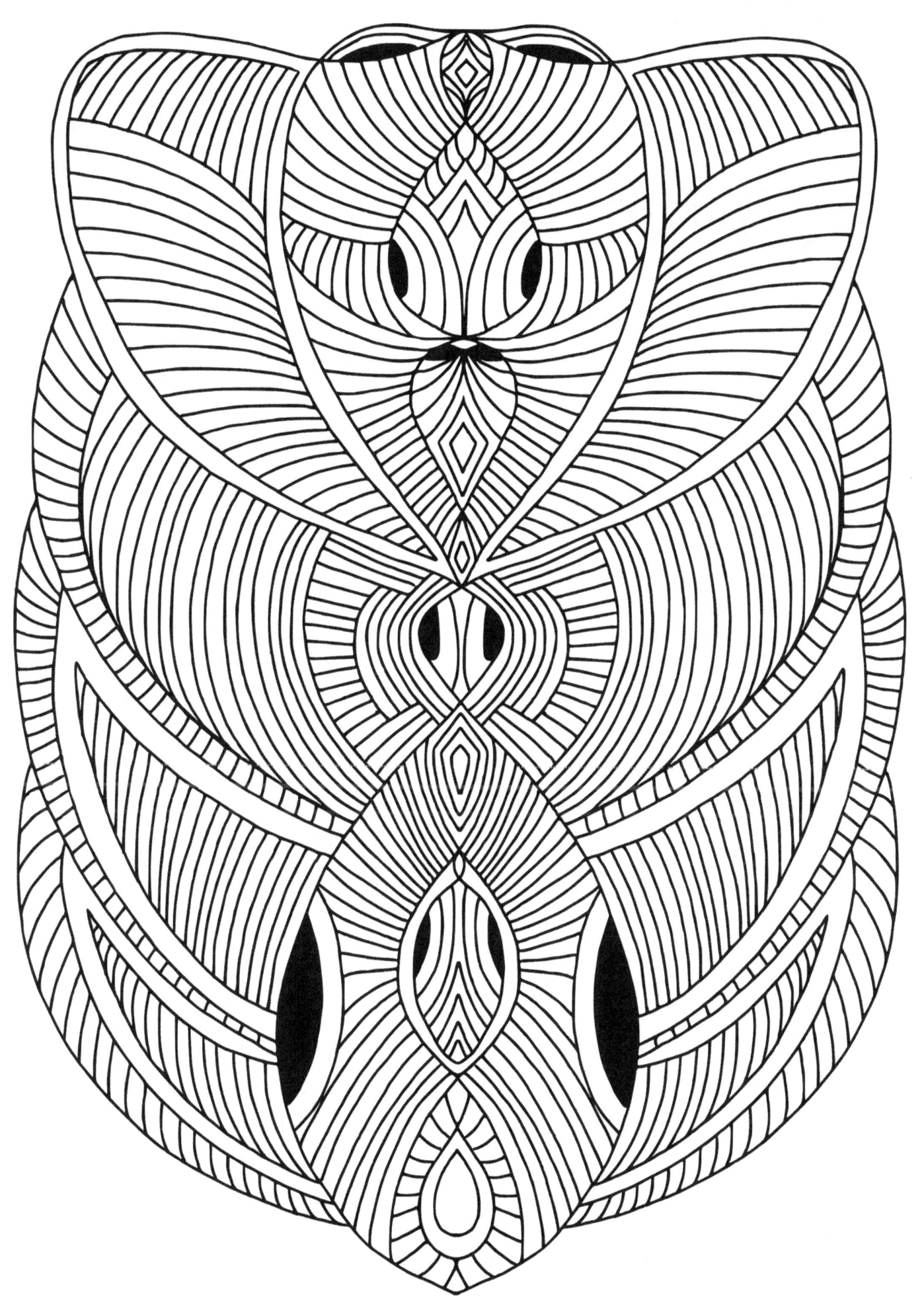

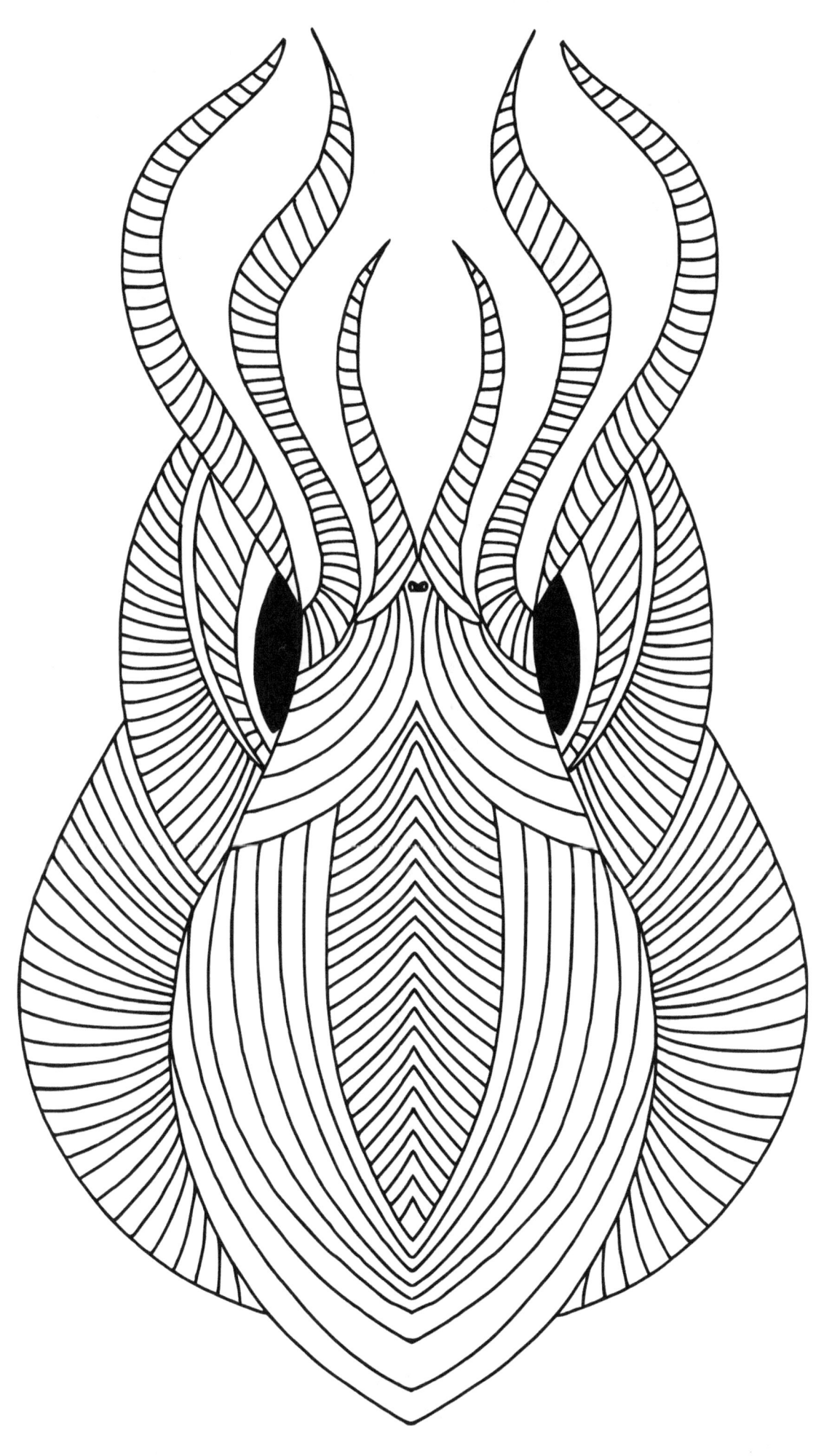

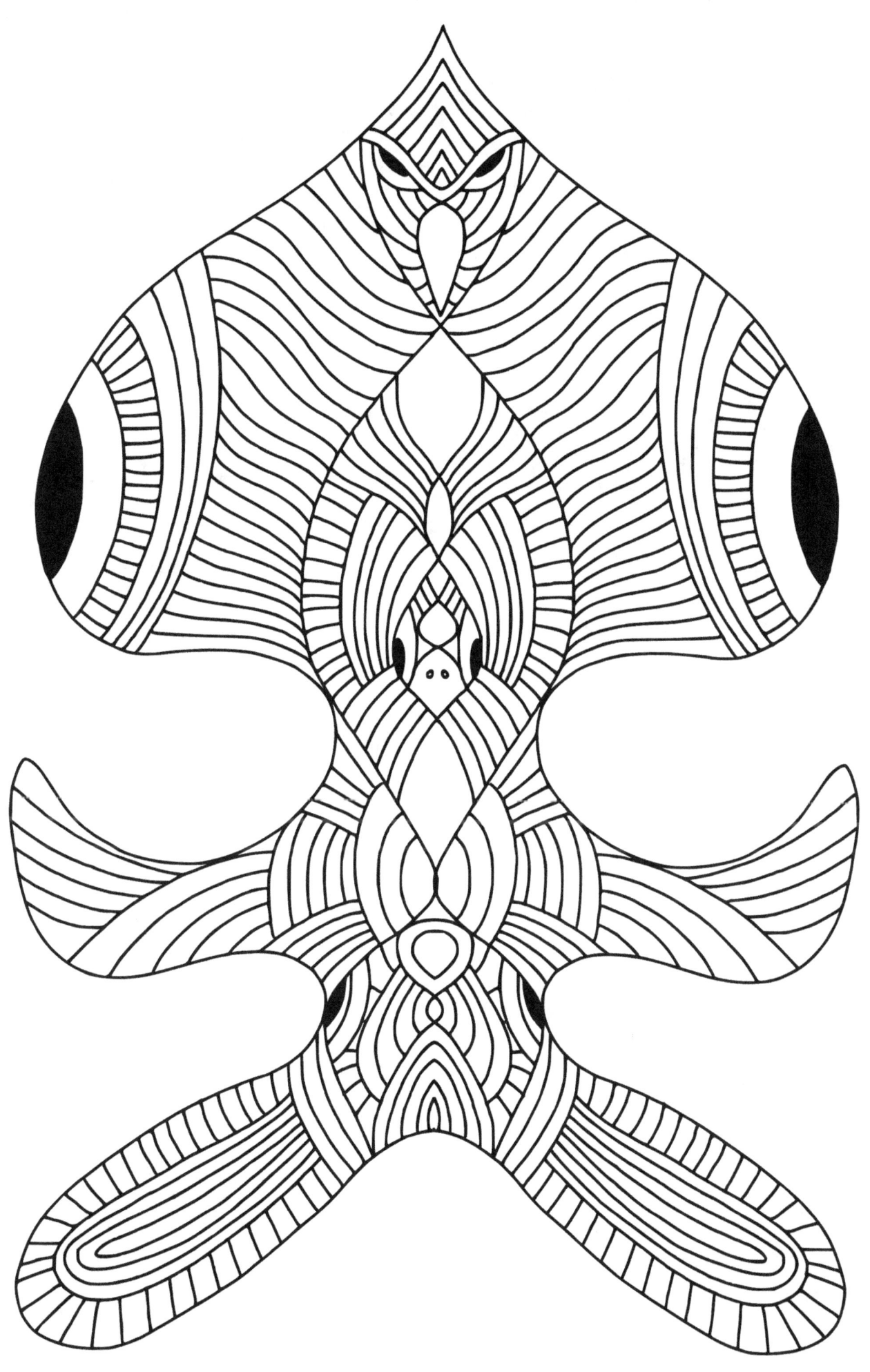

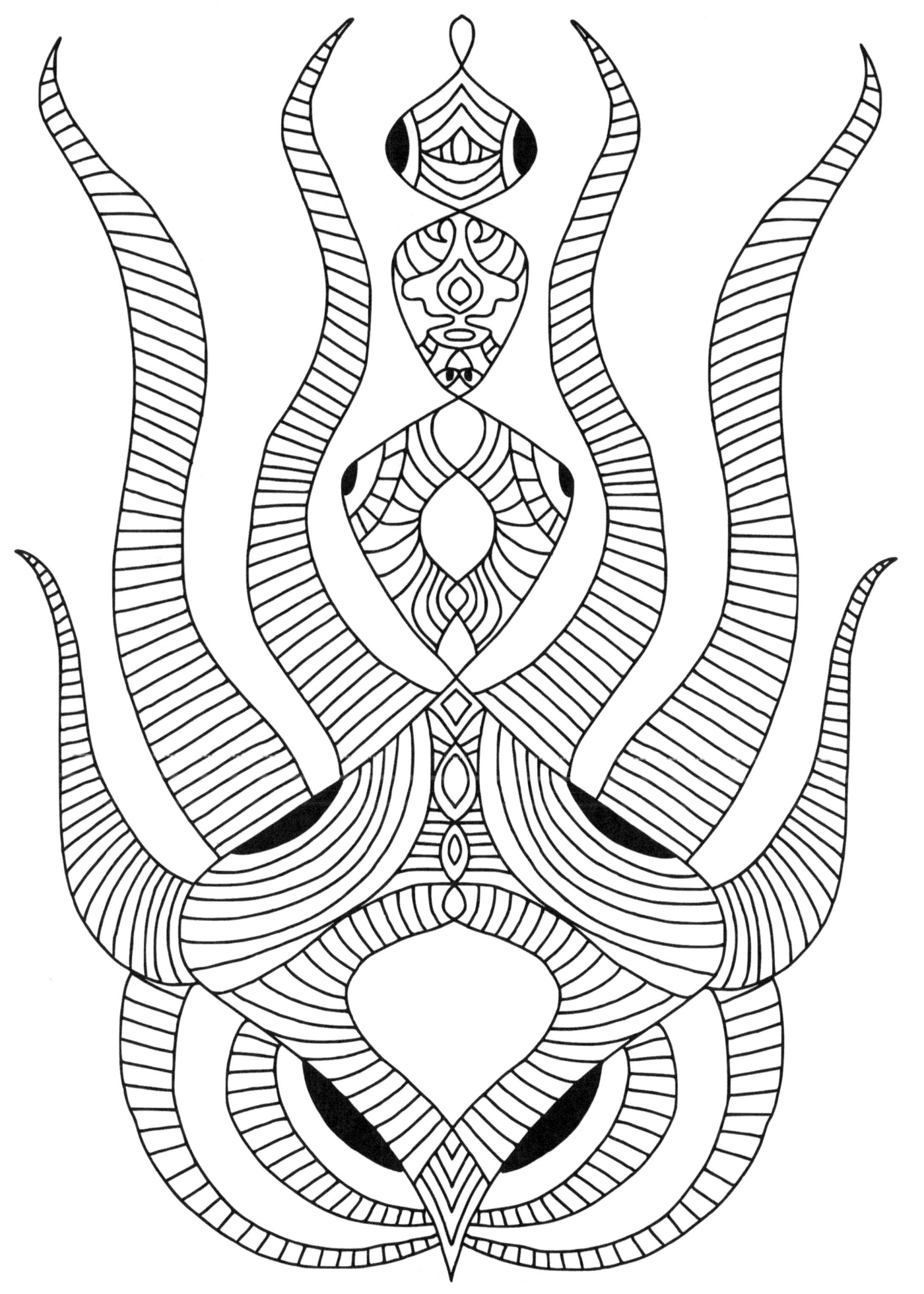

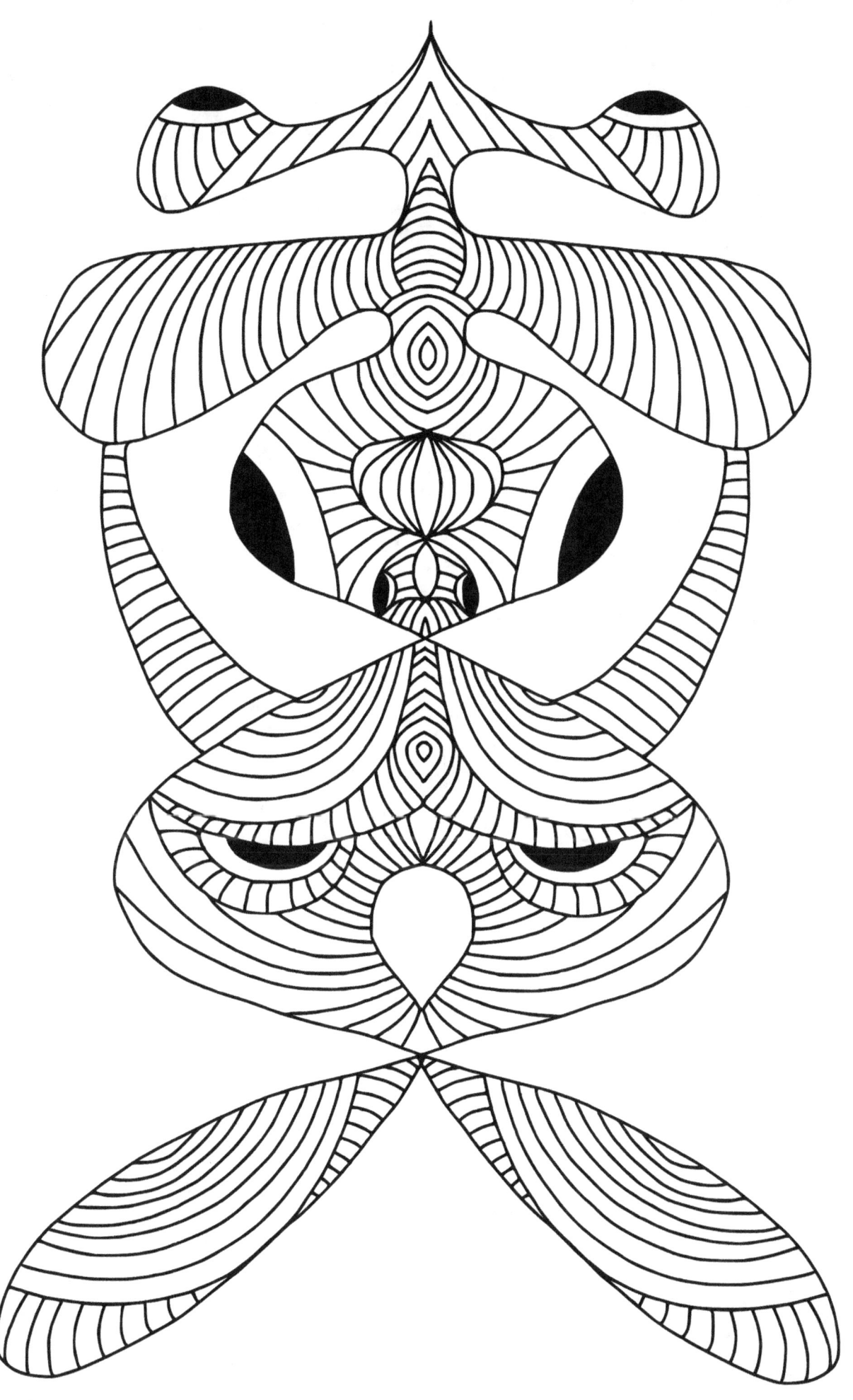

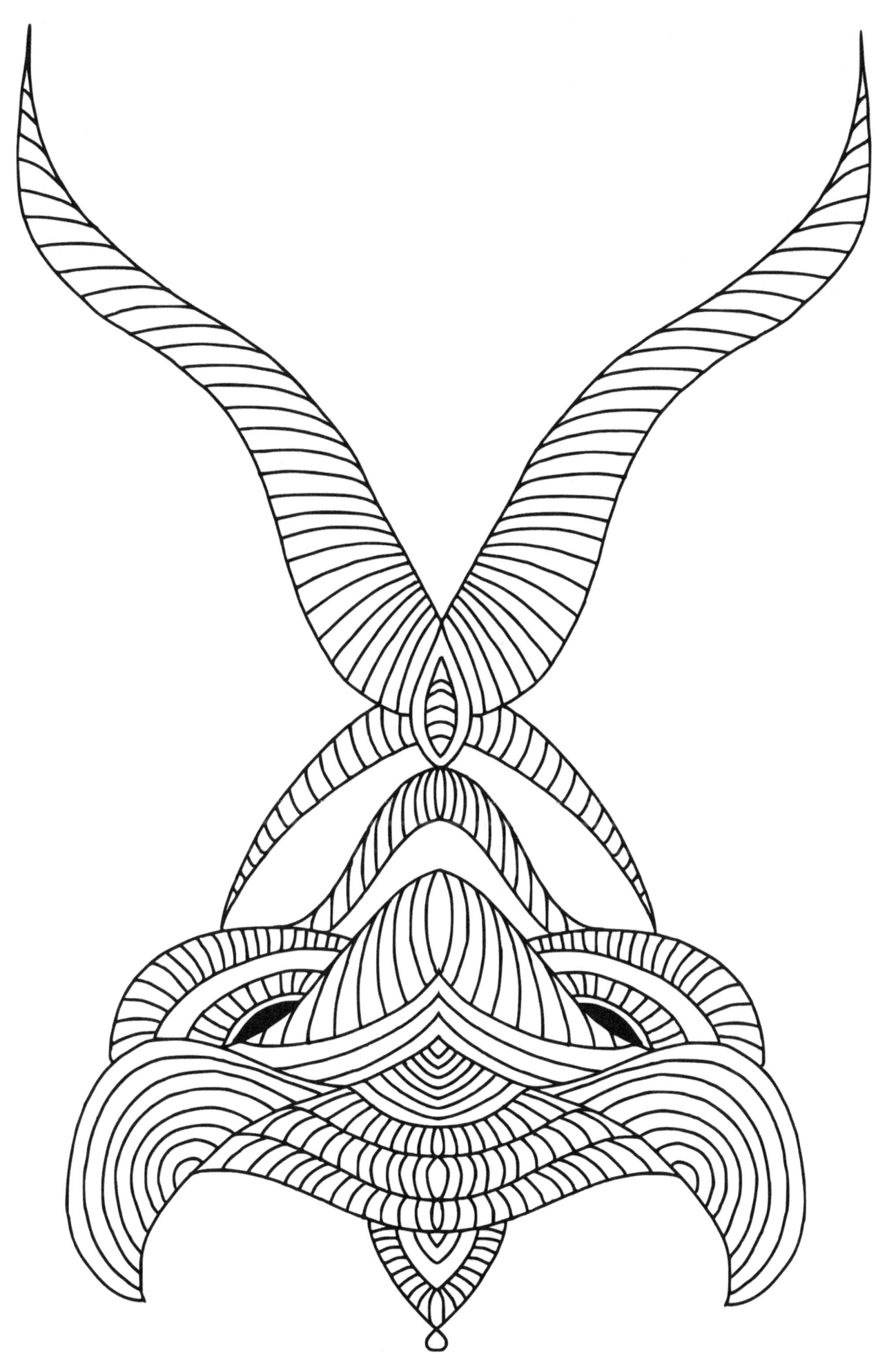

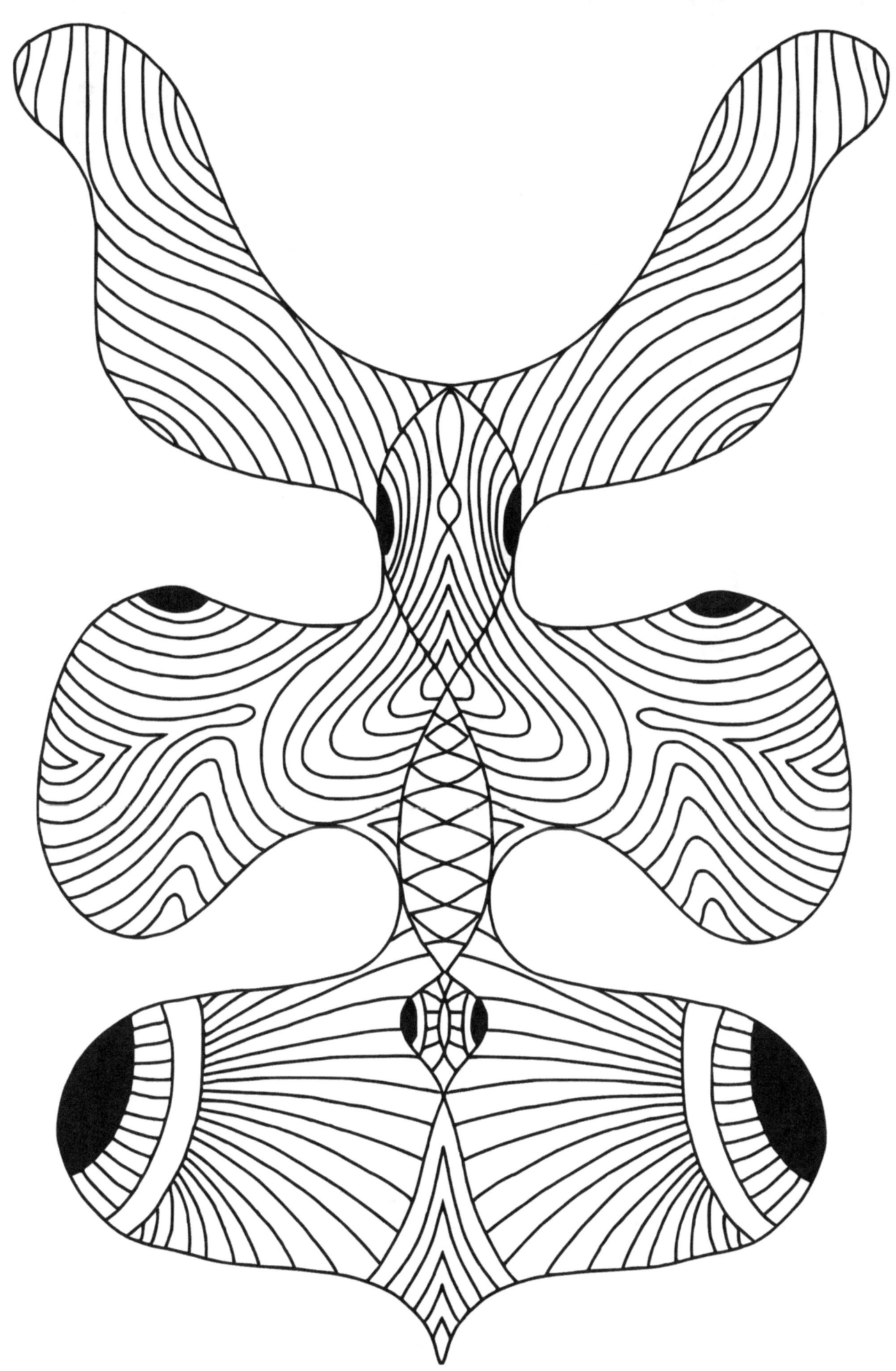

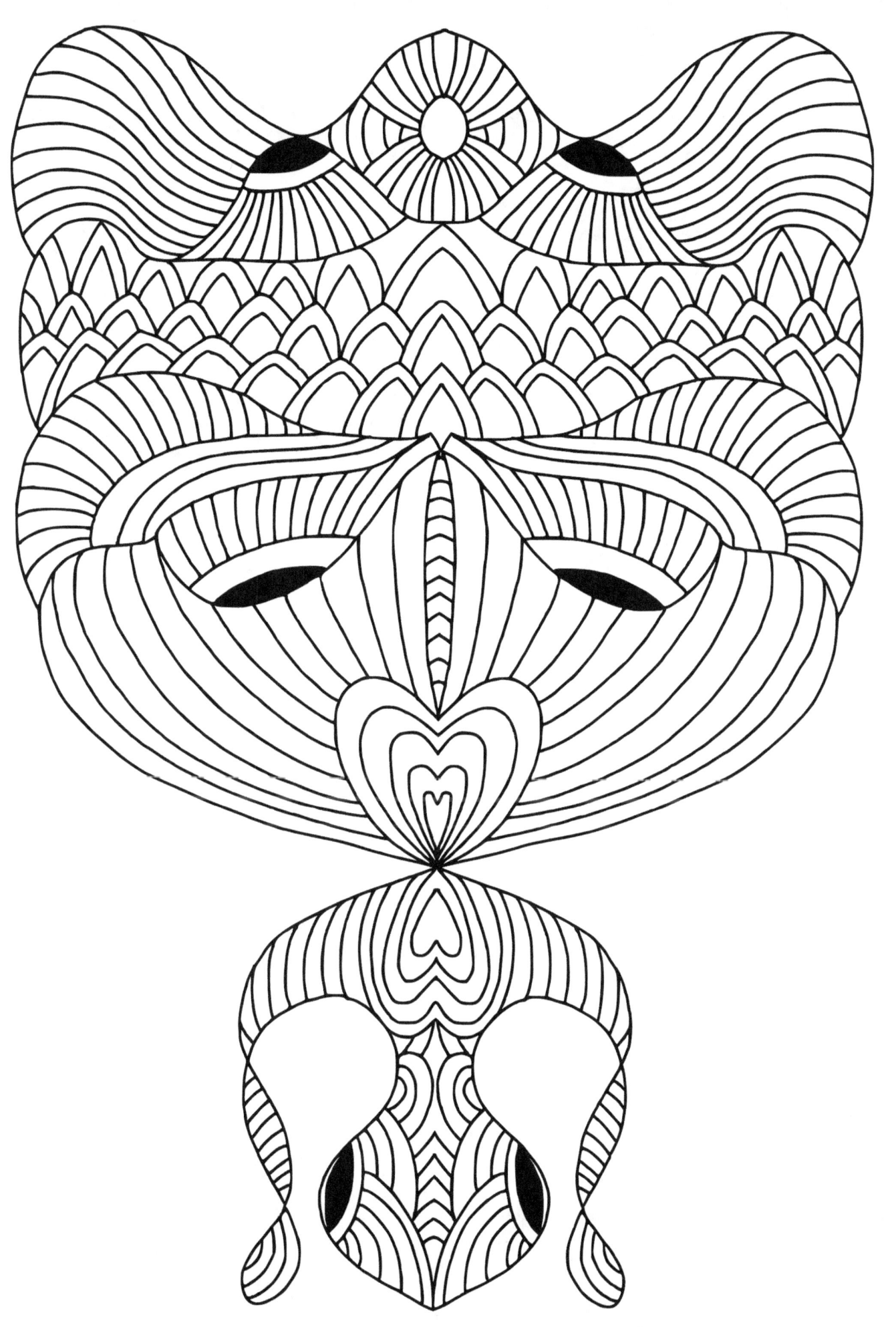

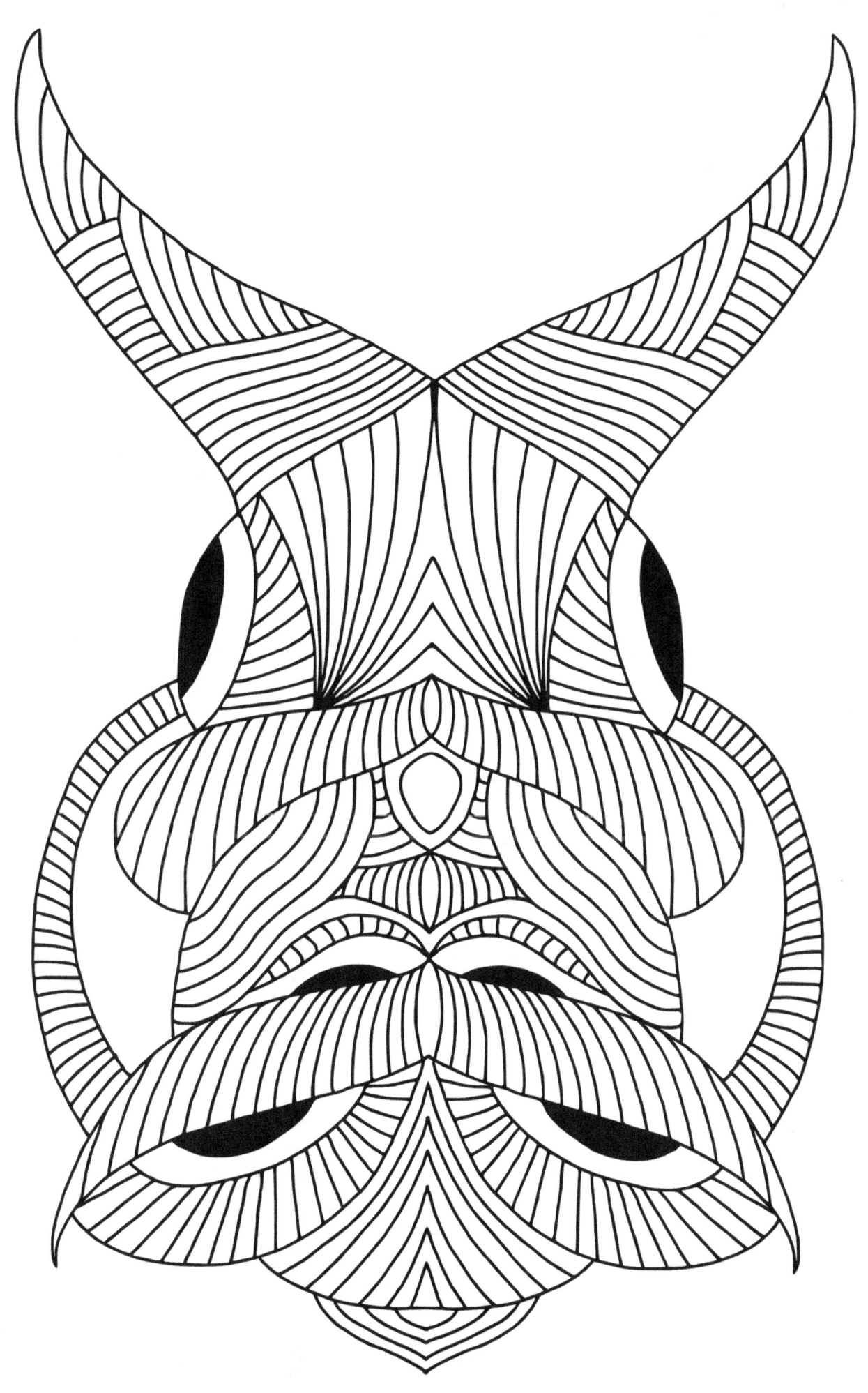

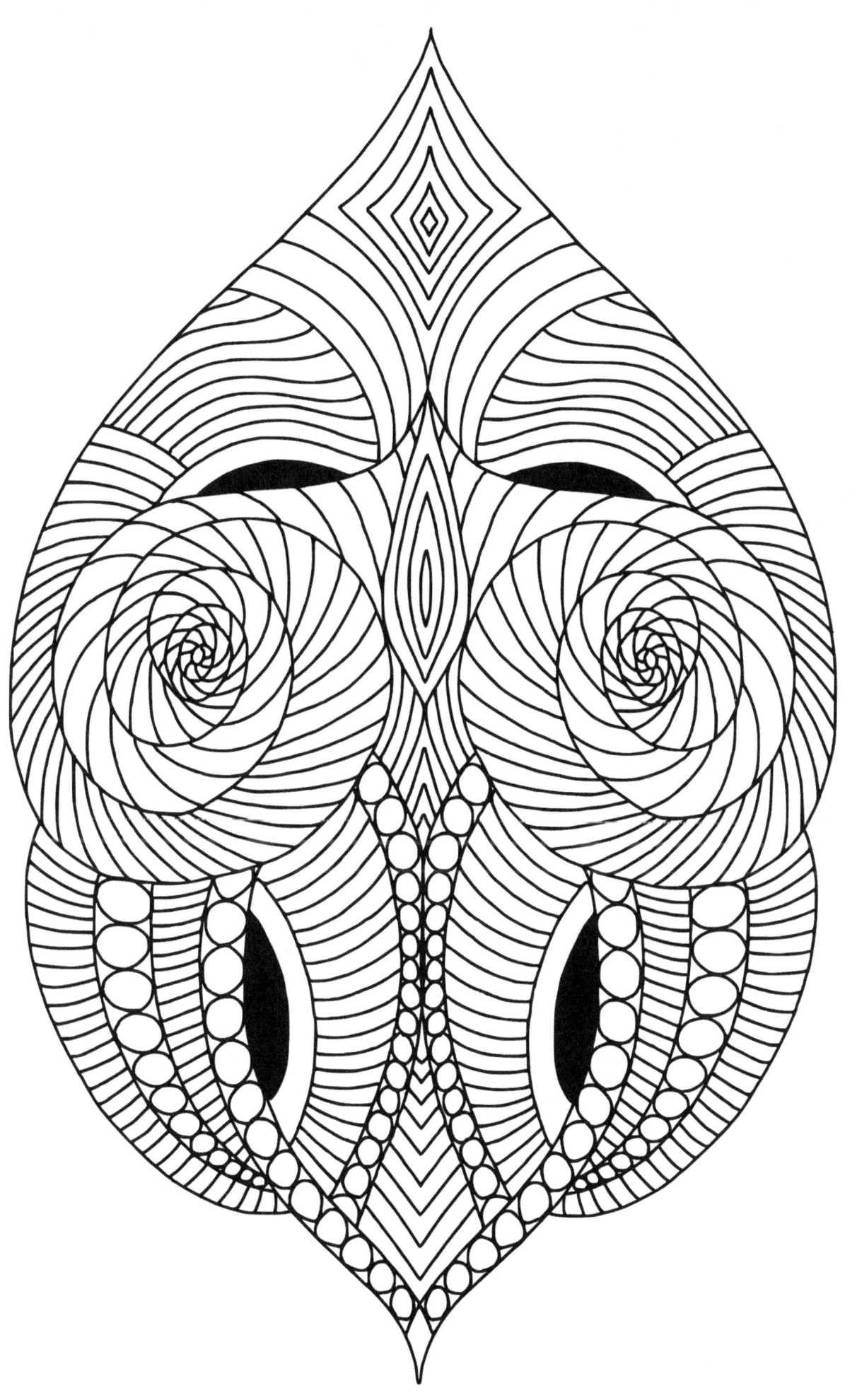

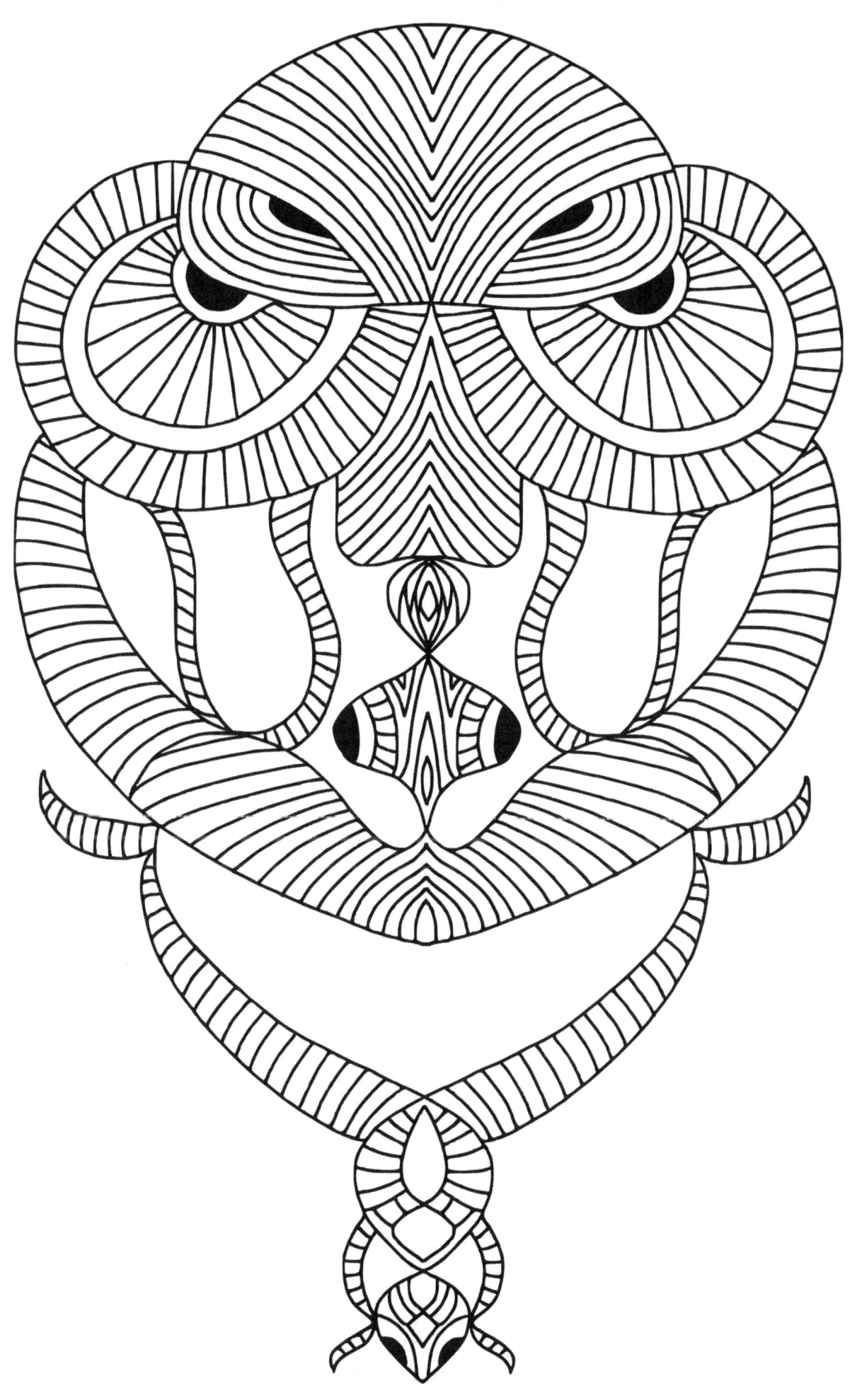

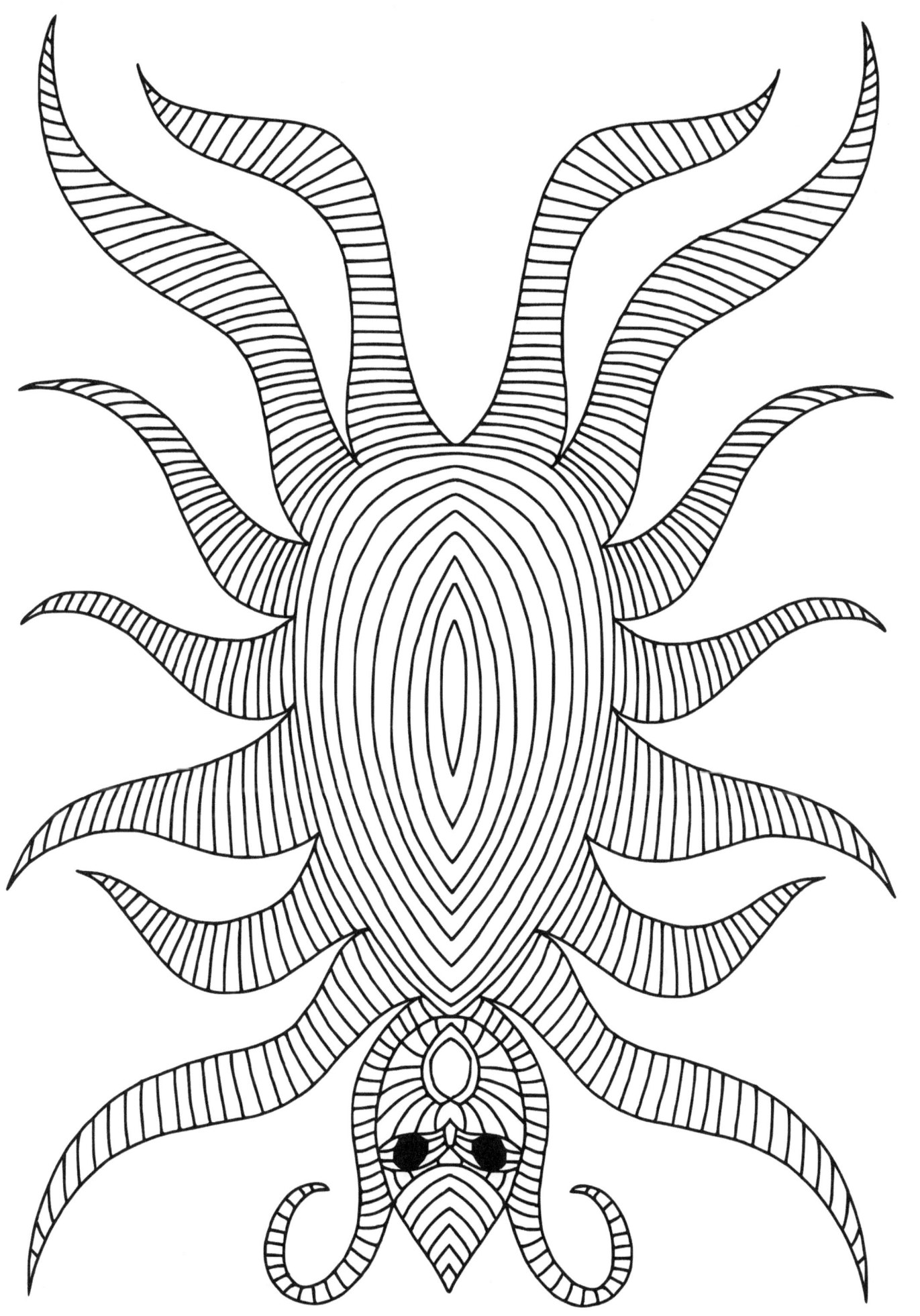

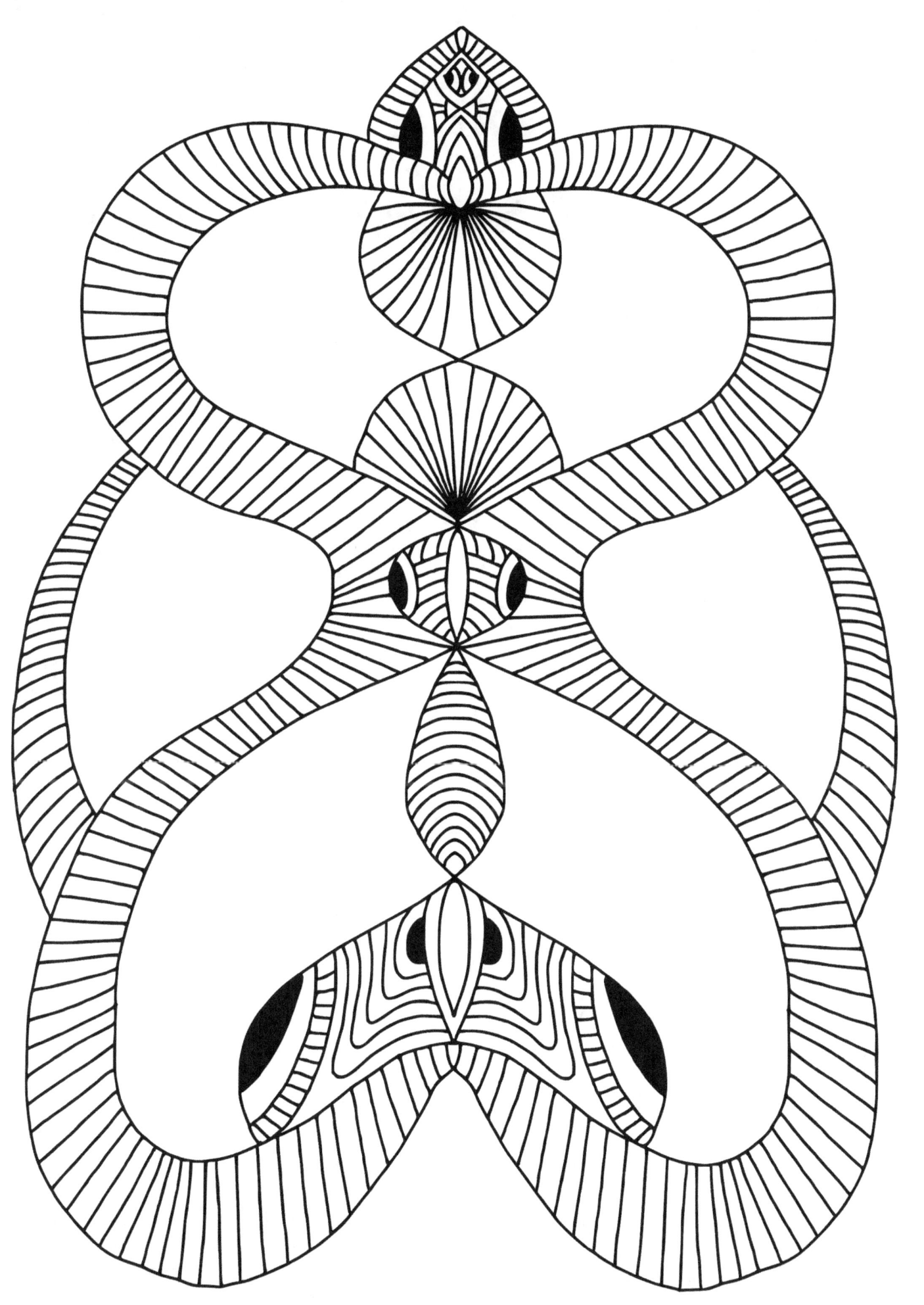

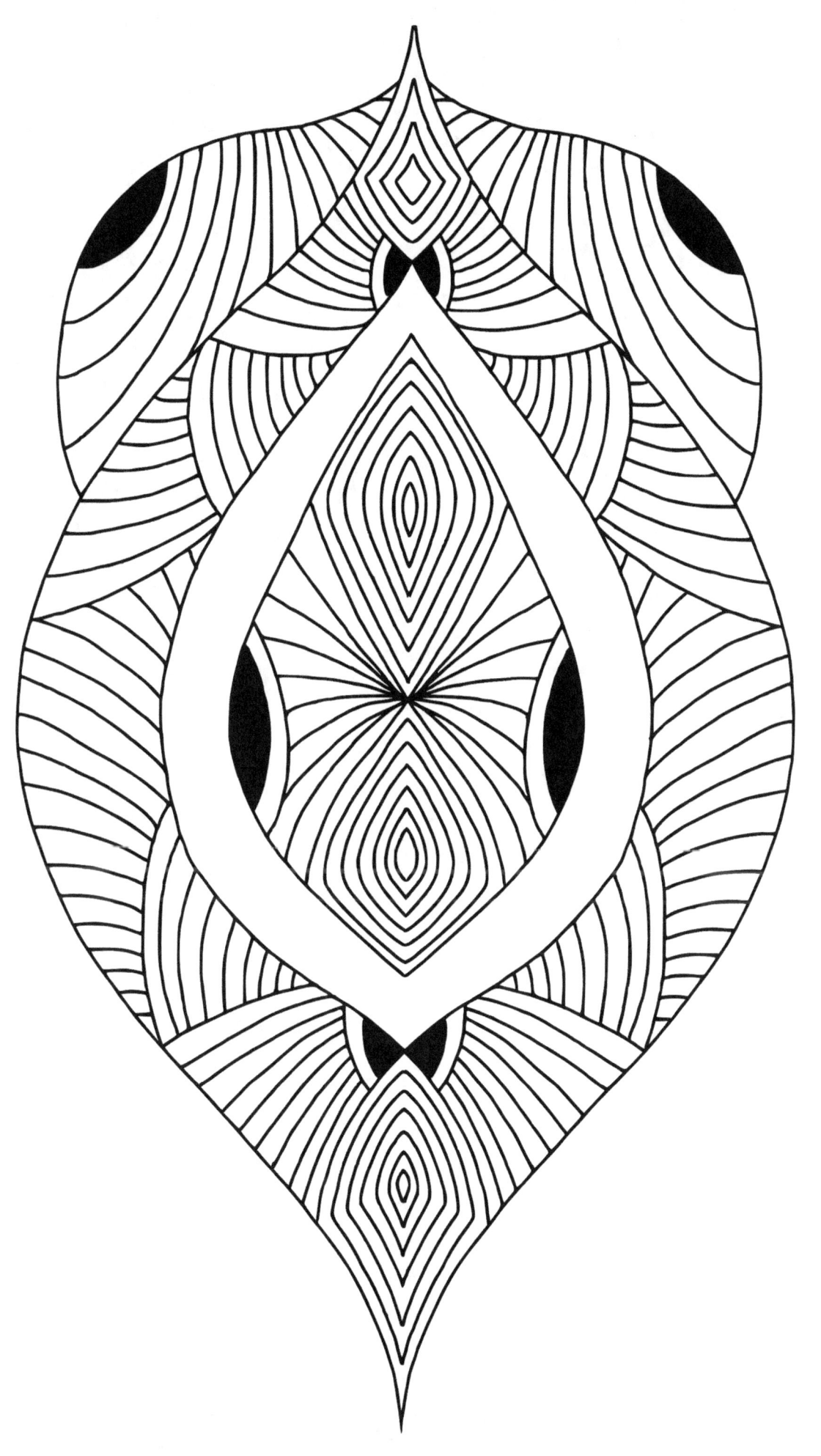

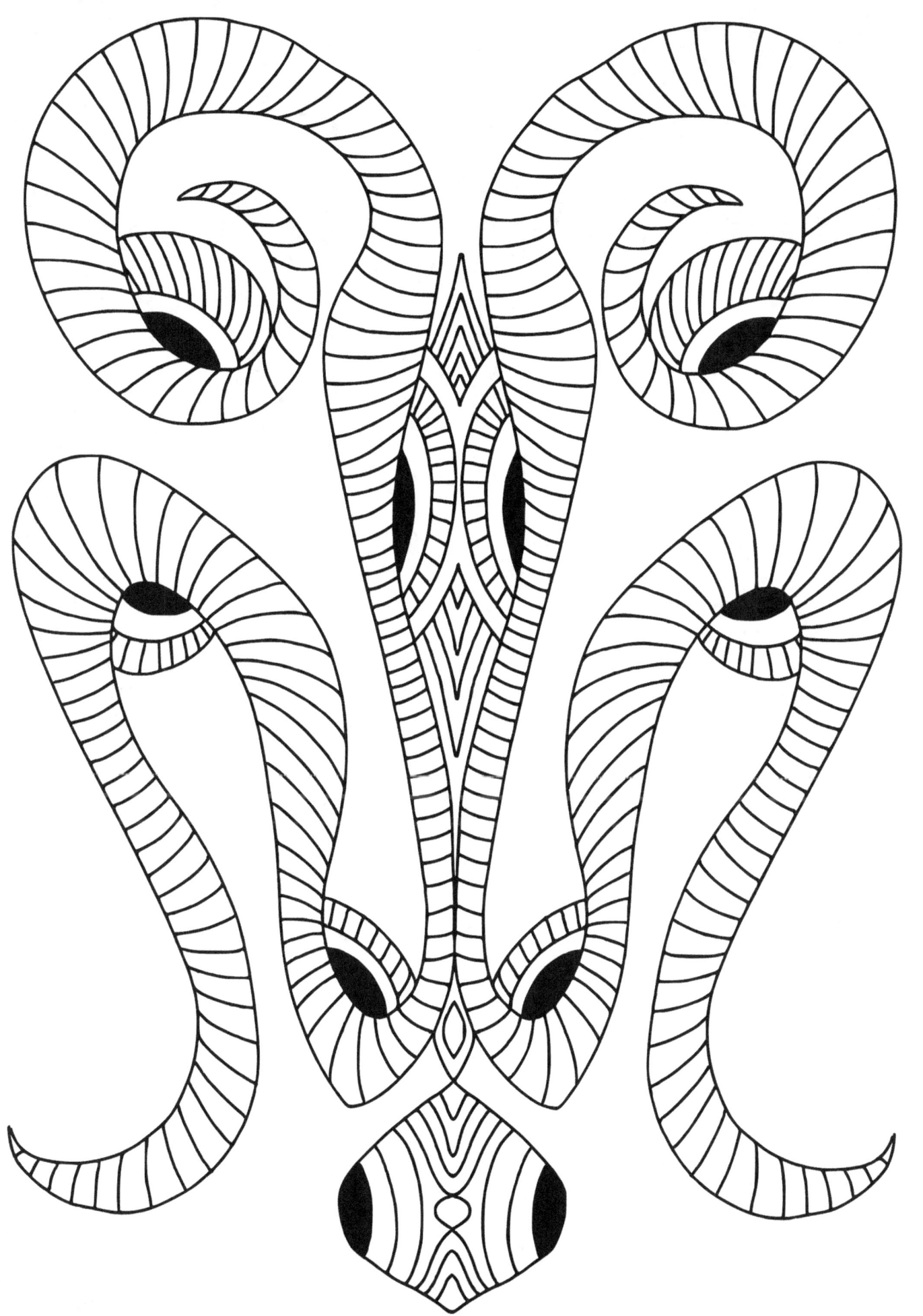

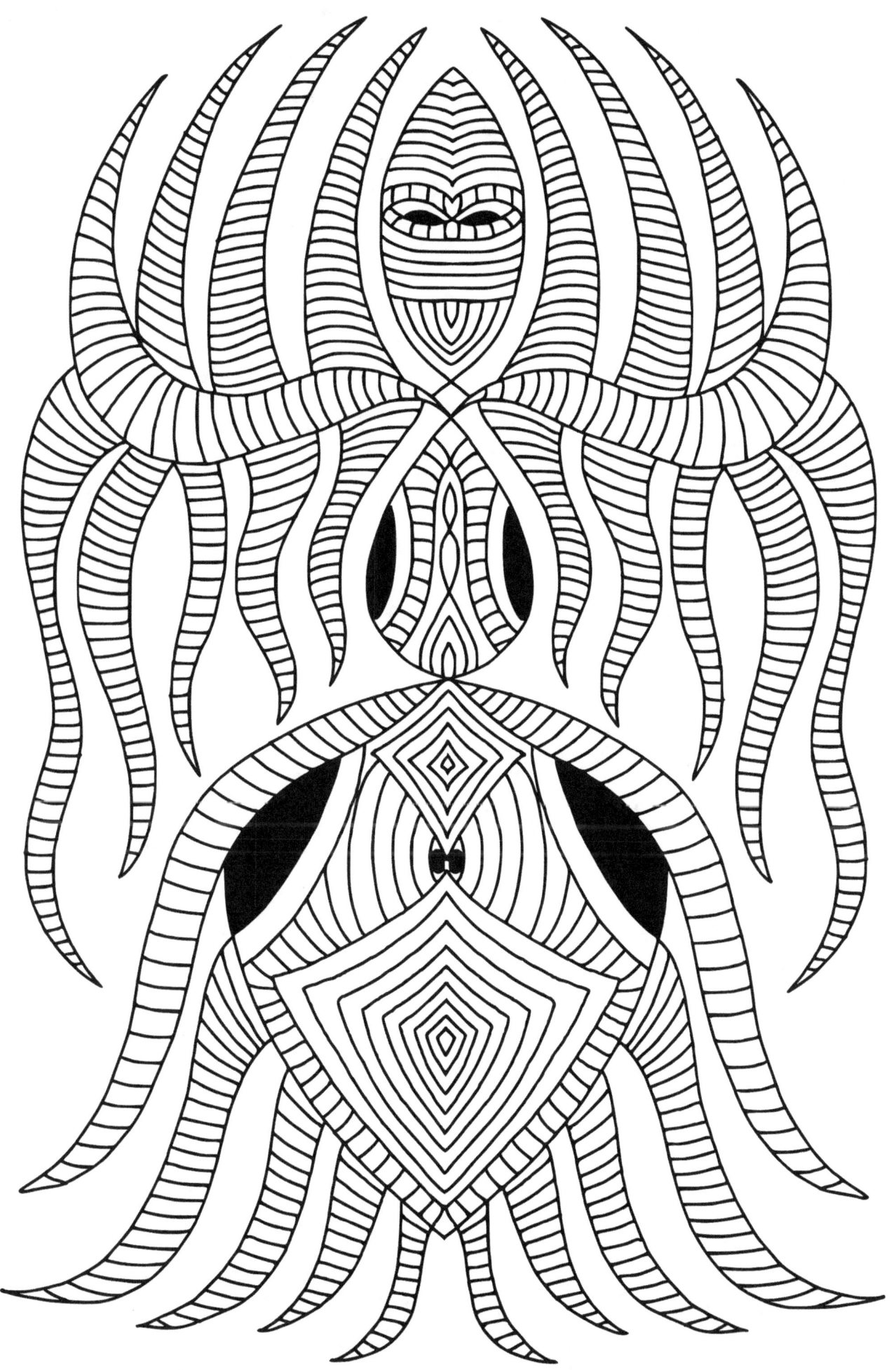

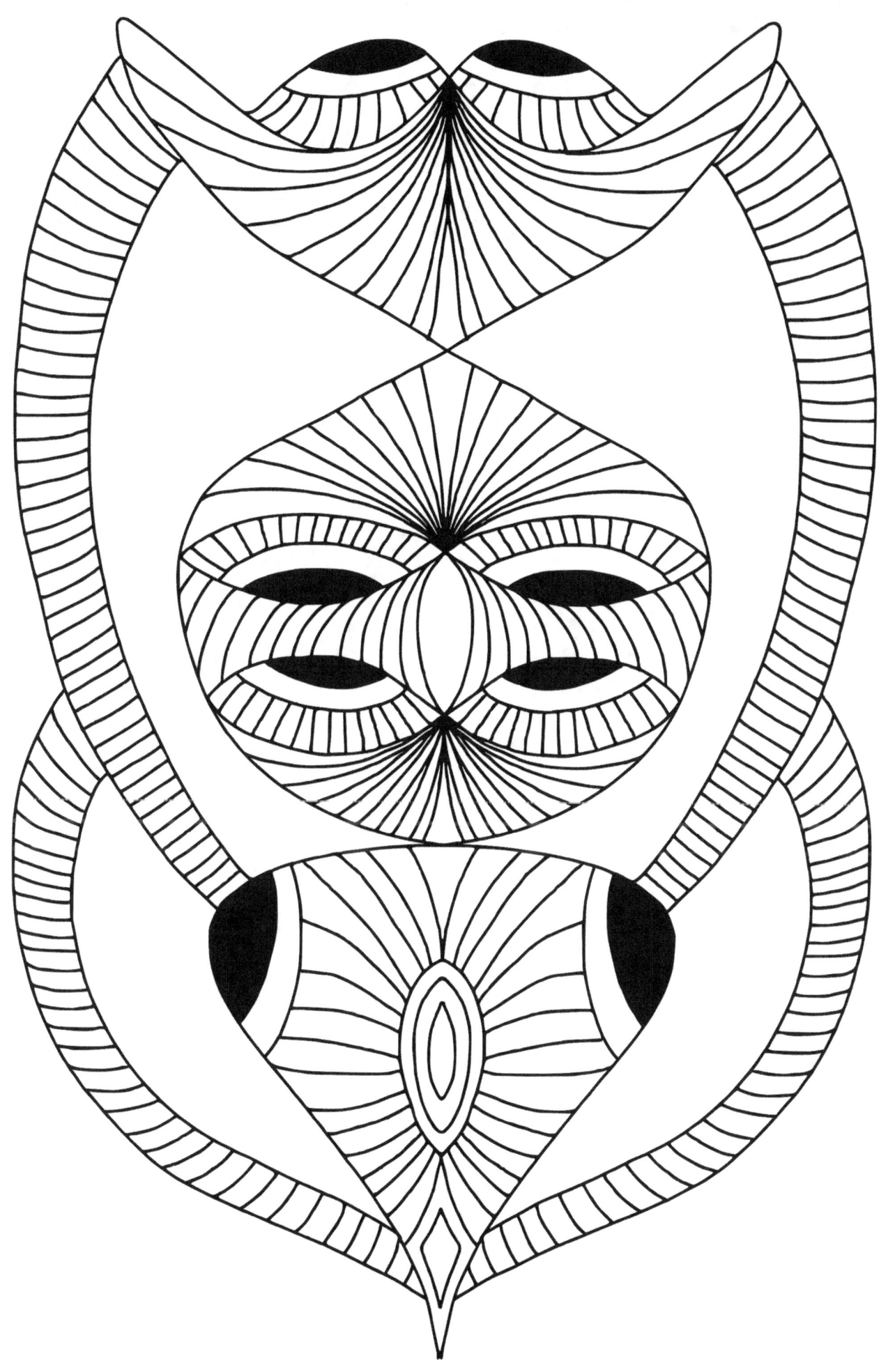

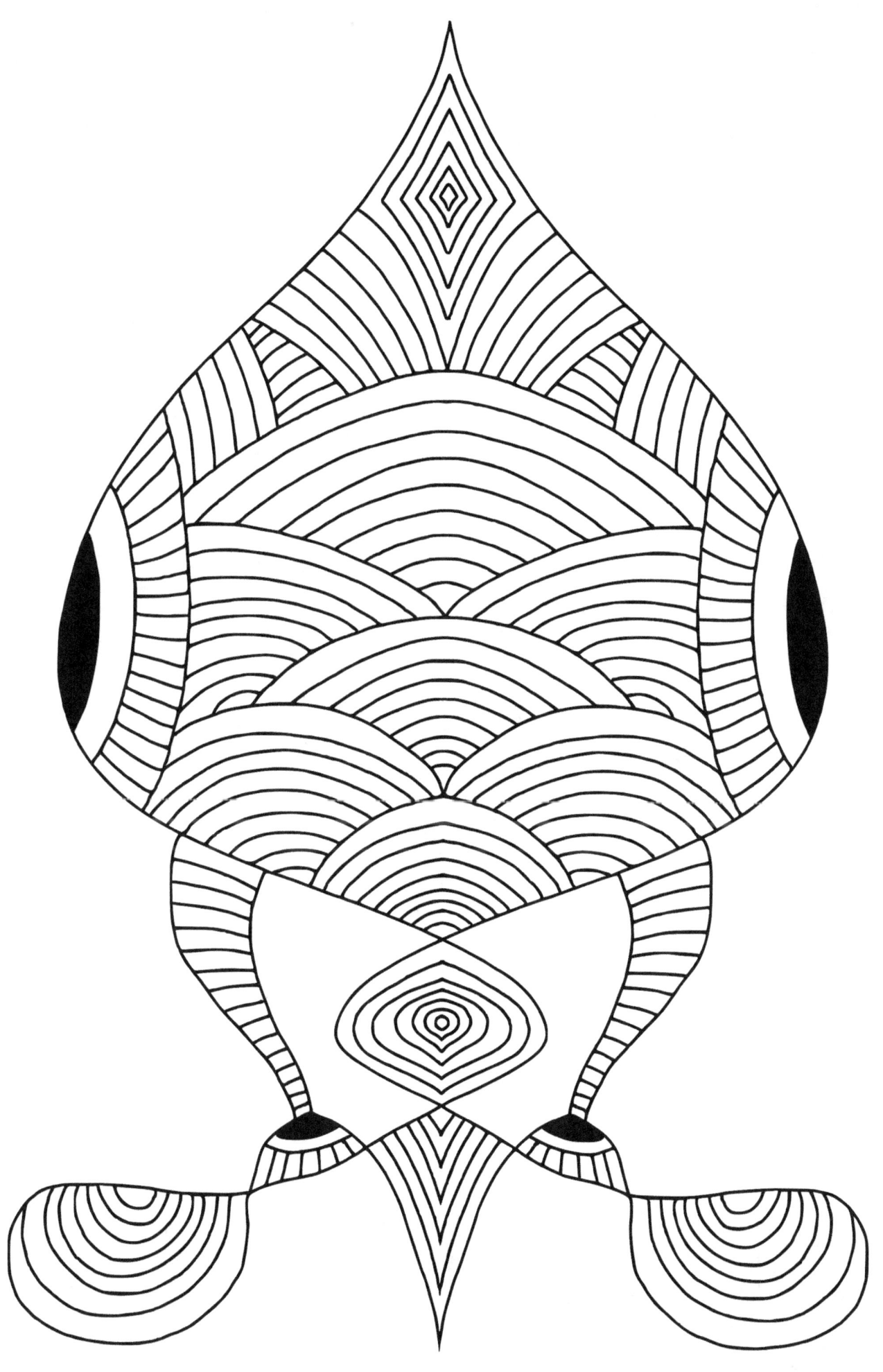

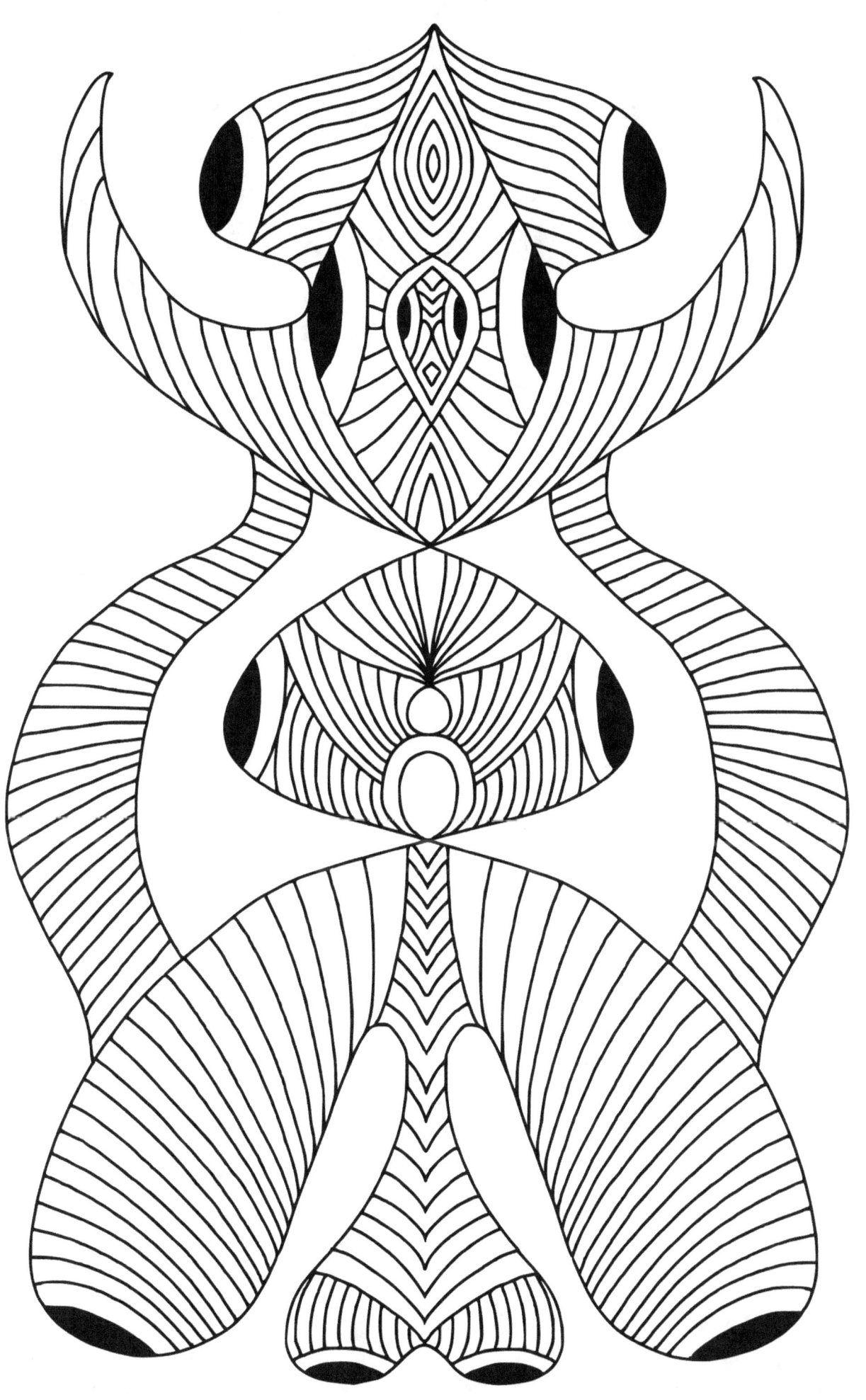

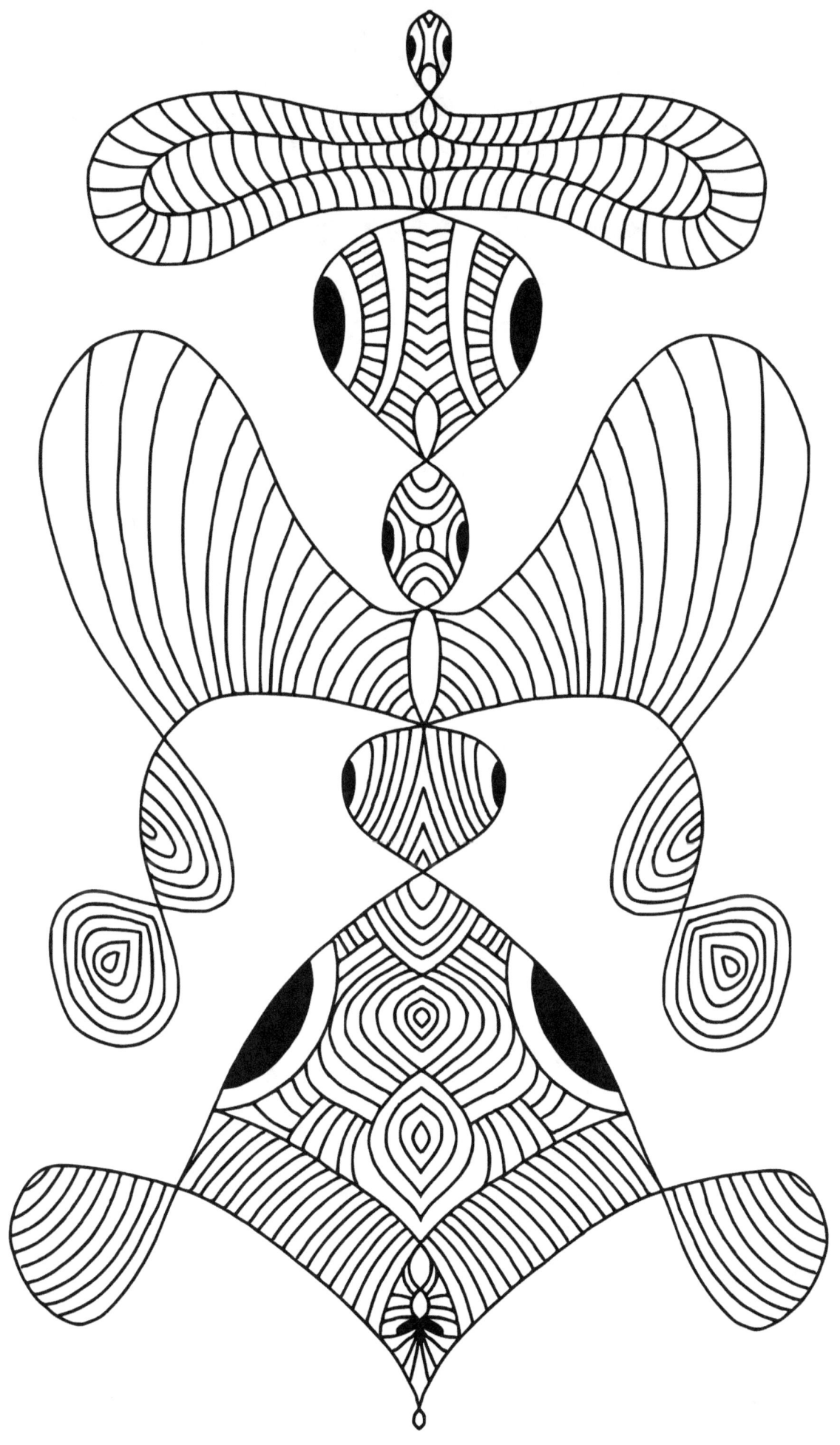

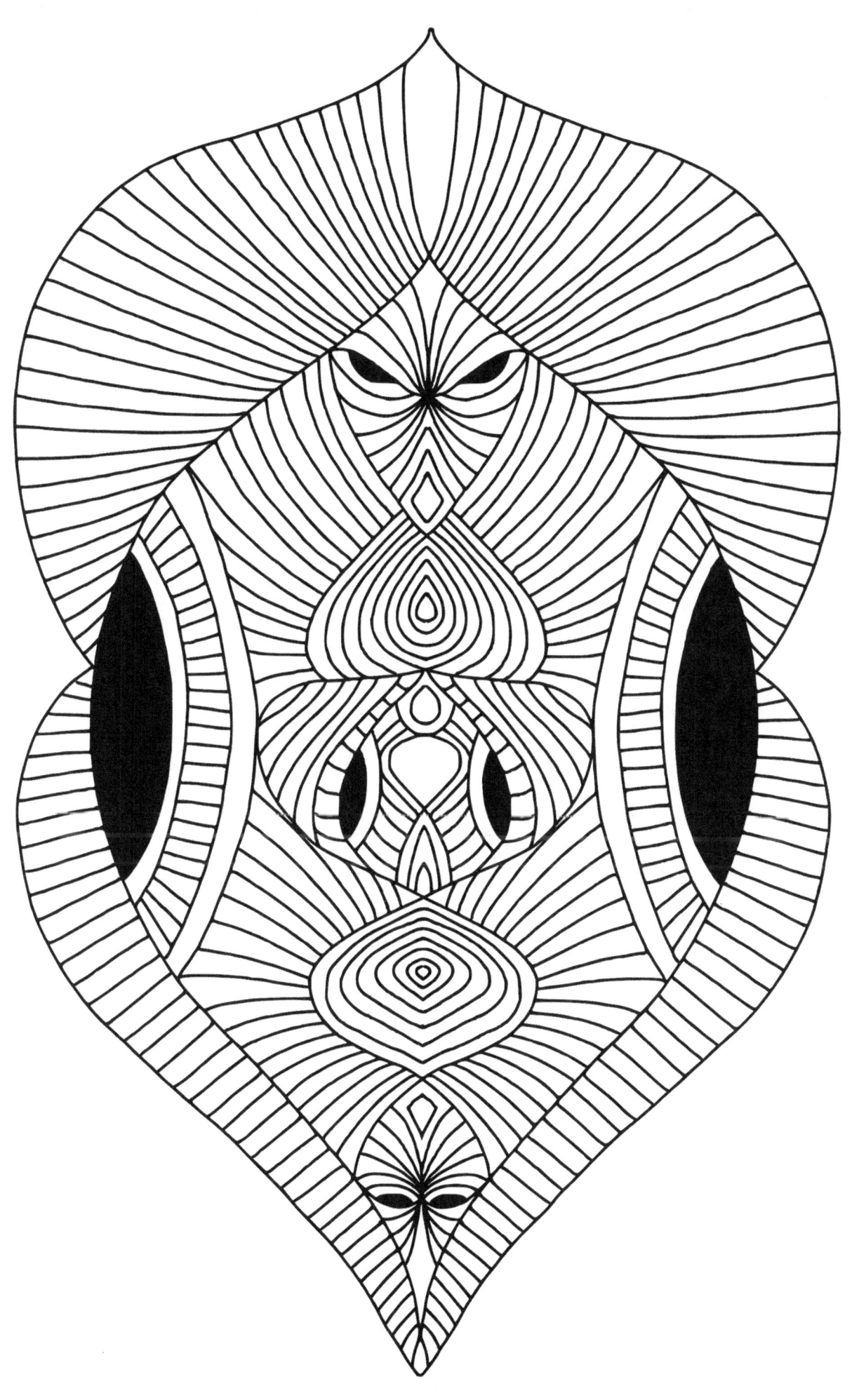

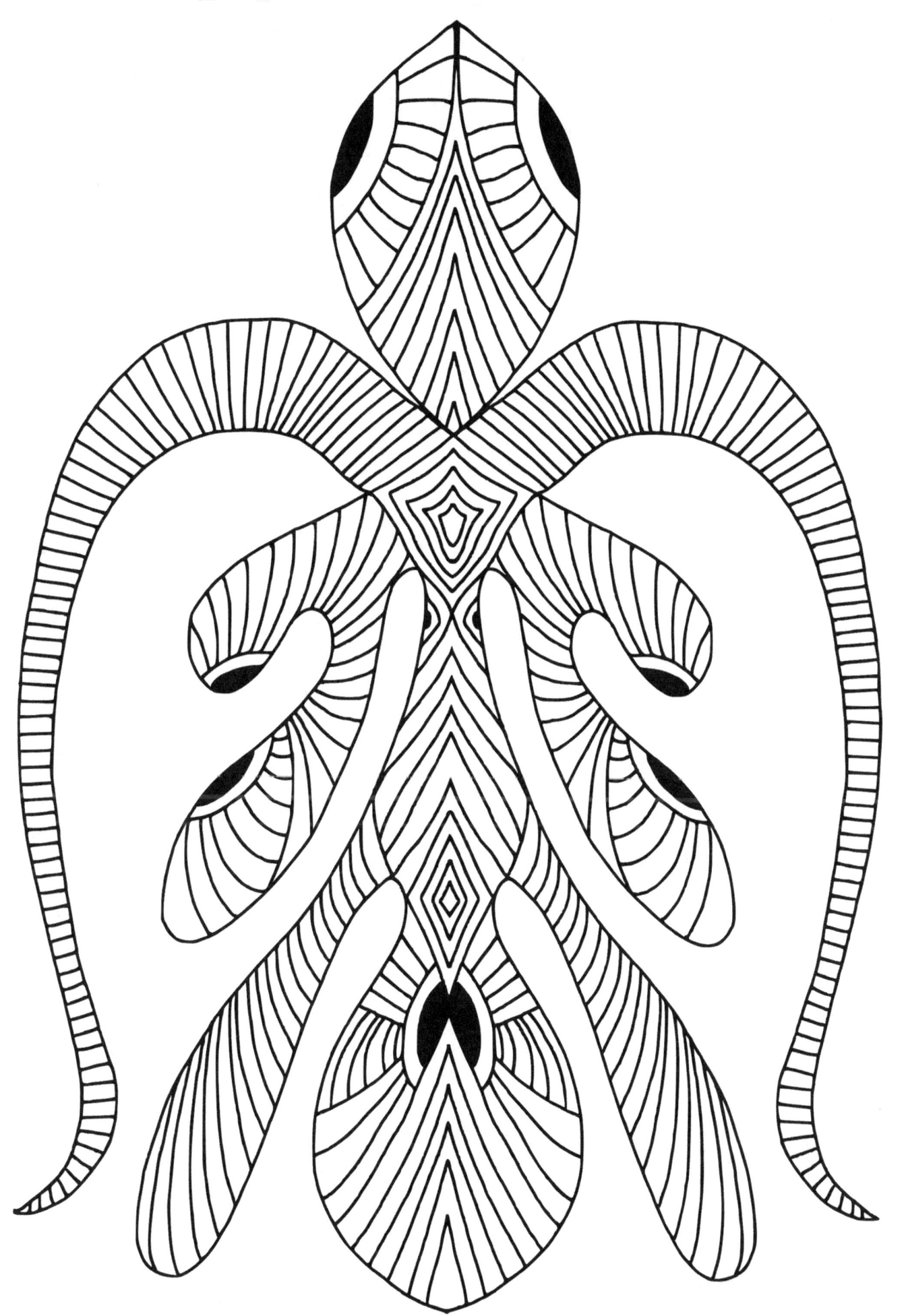

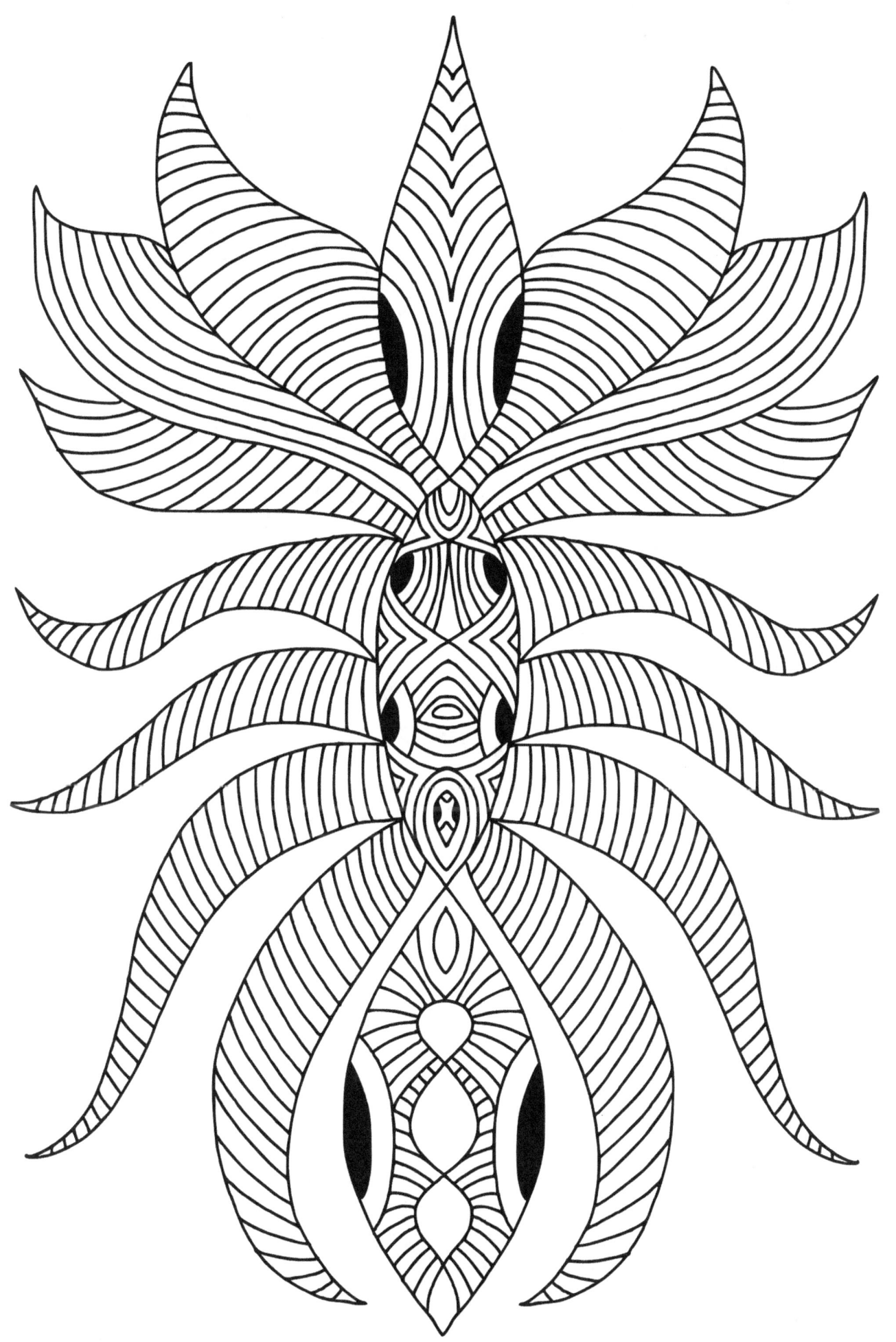

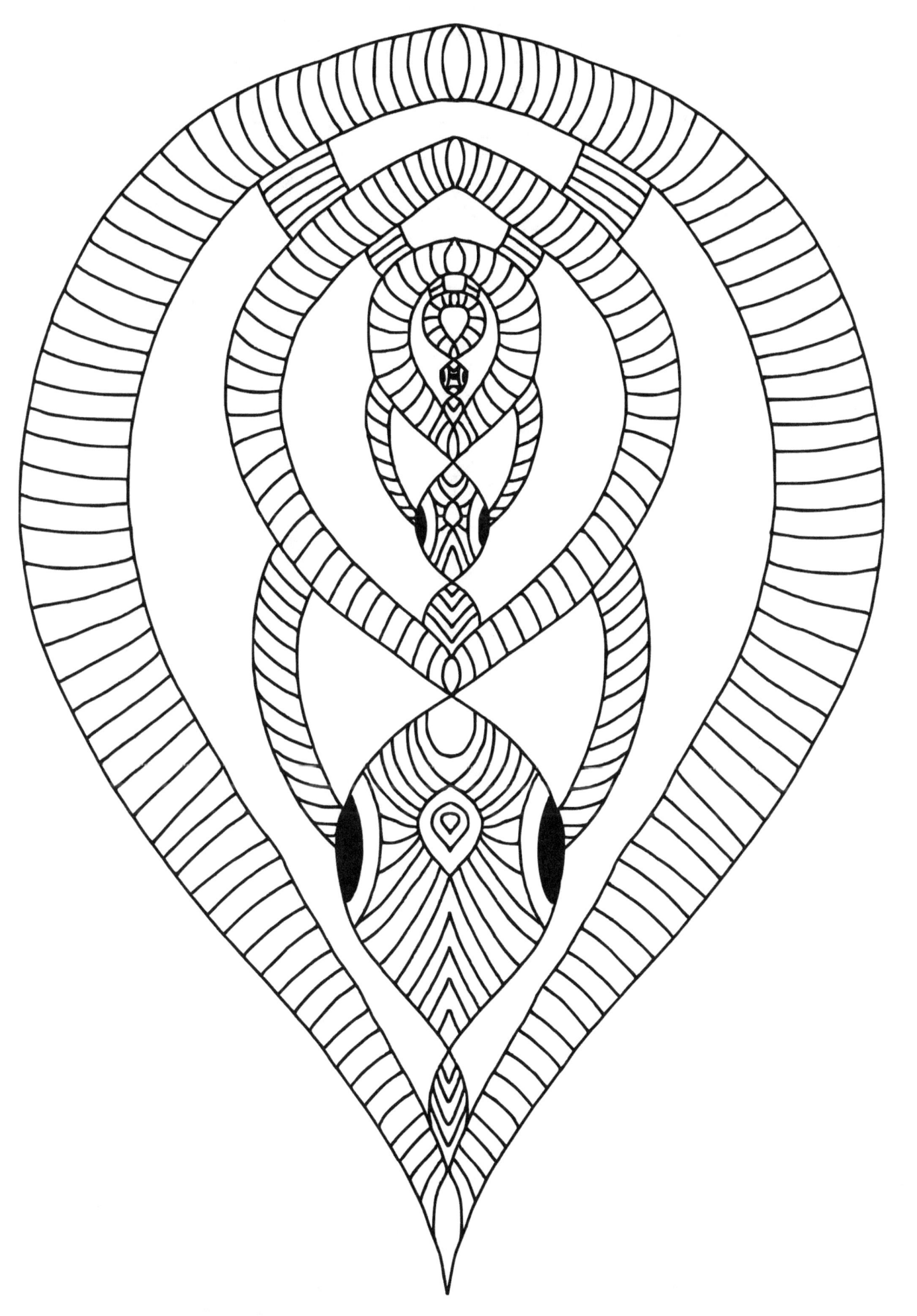

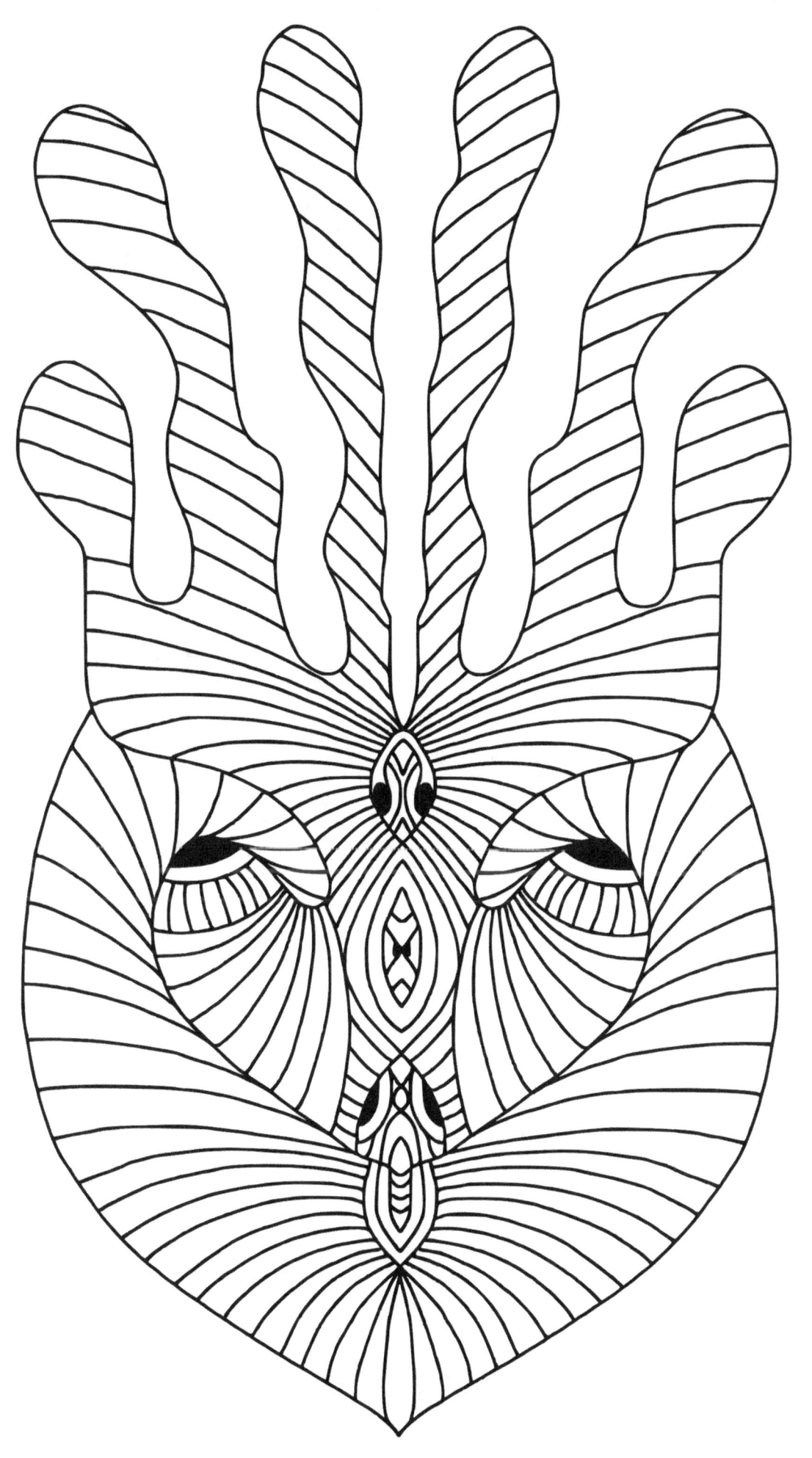

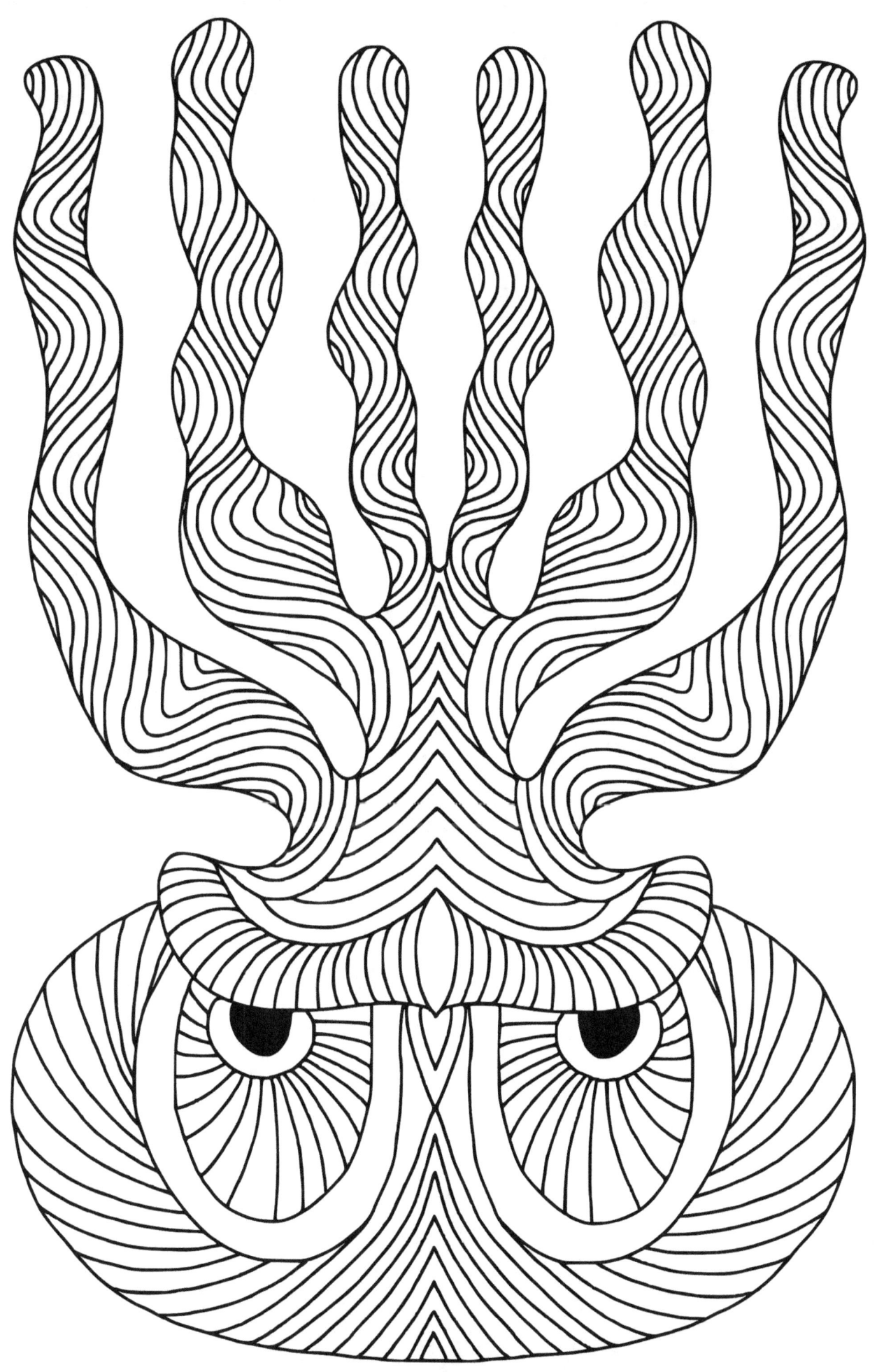

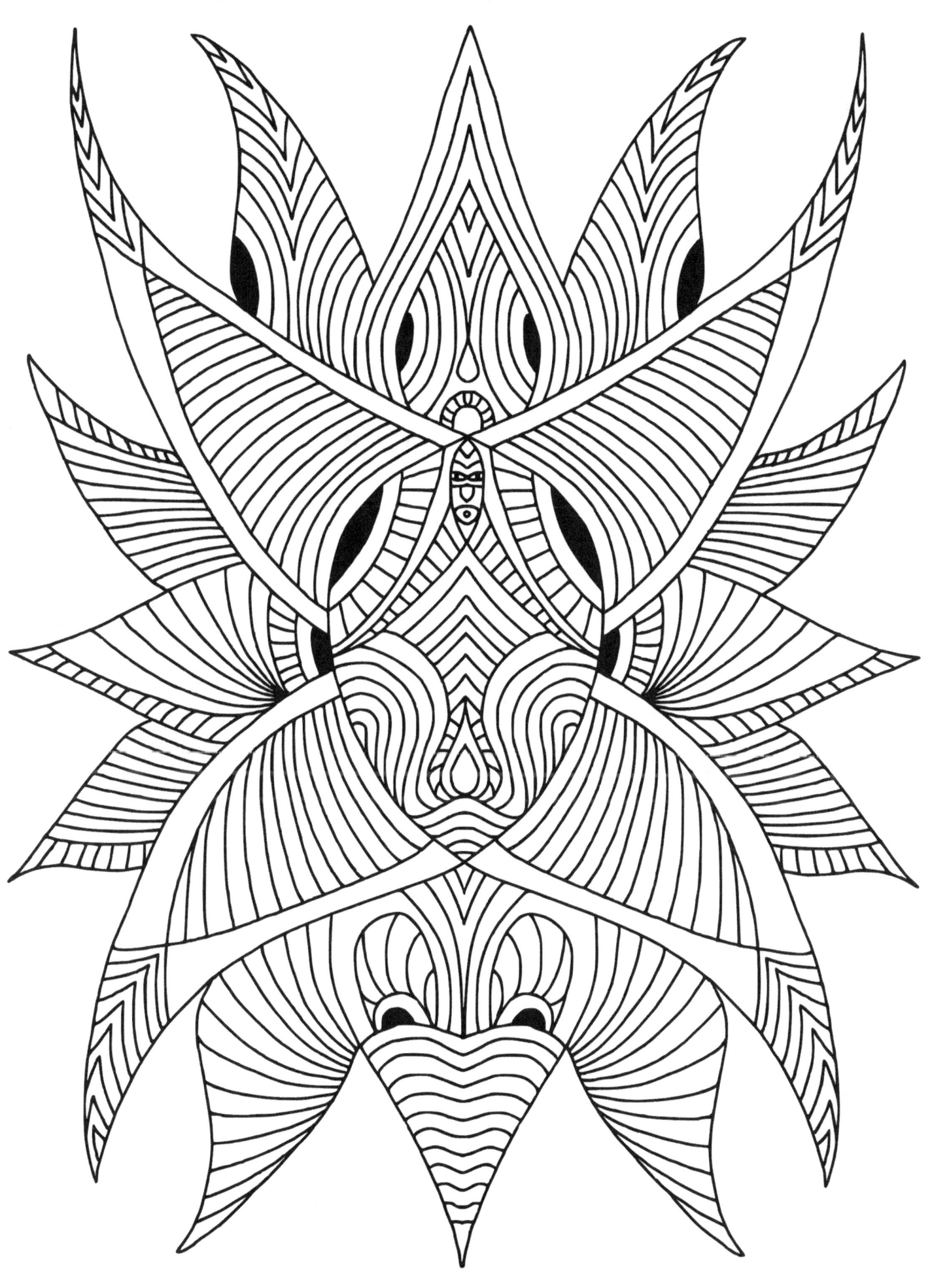

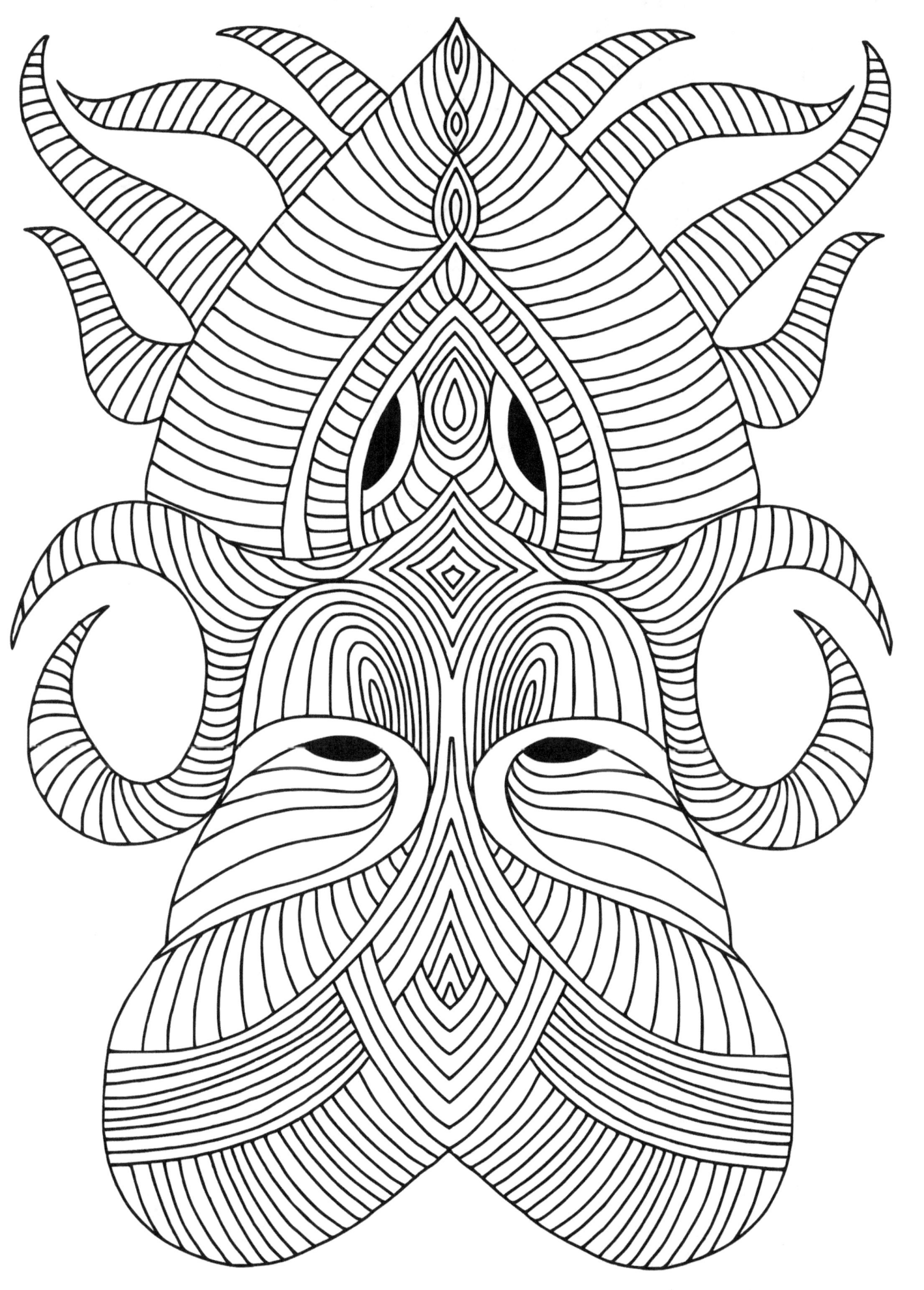

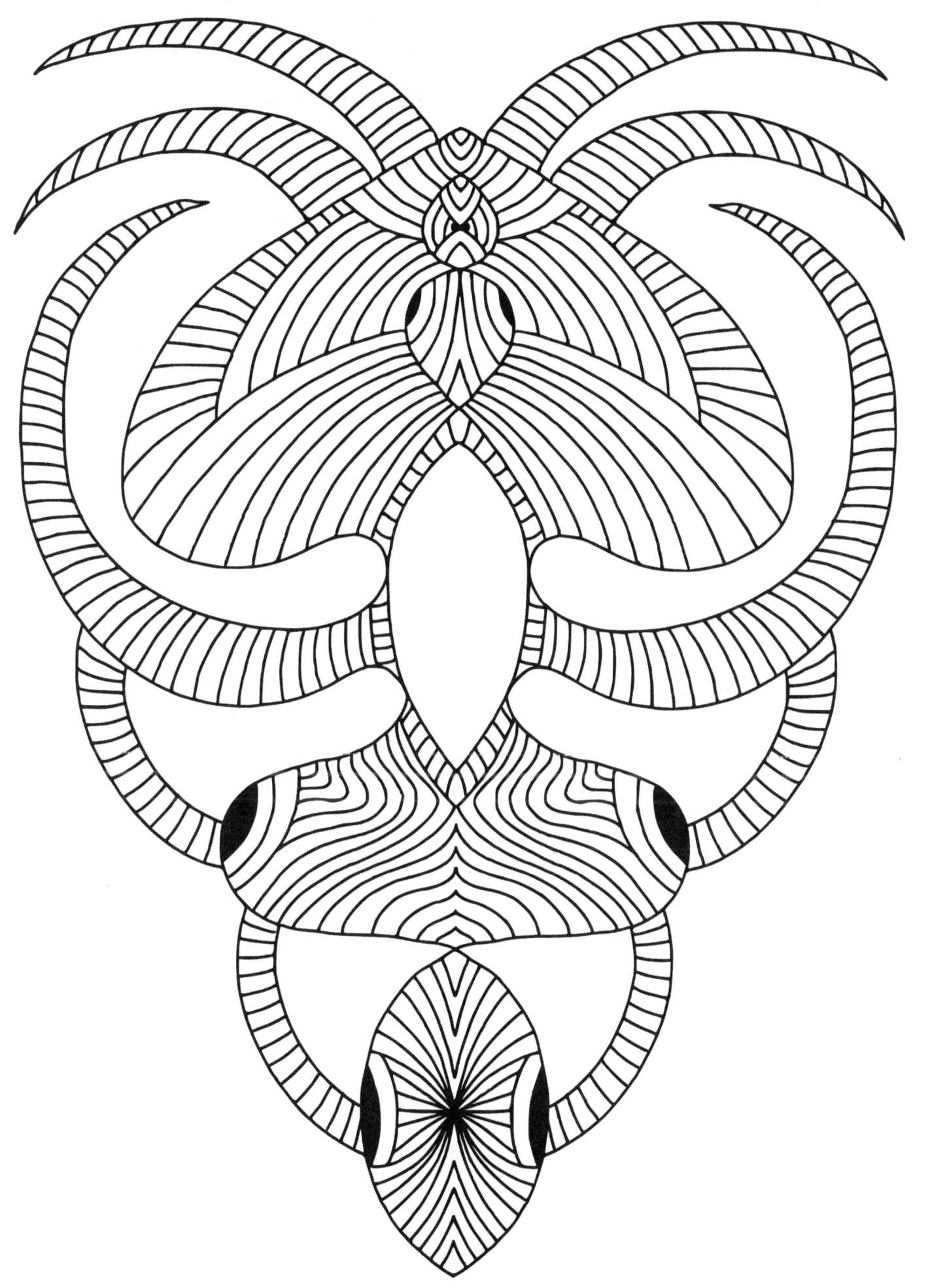

Test your colors here on the samples from
"My Pocket Coloring Companion"
&
"My Coloring Companion"

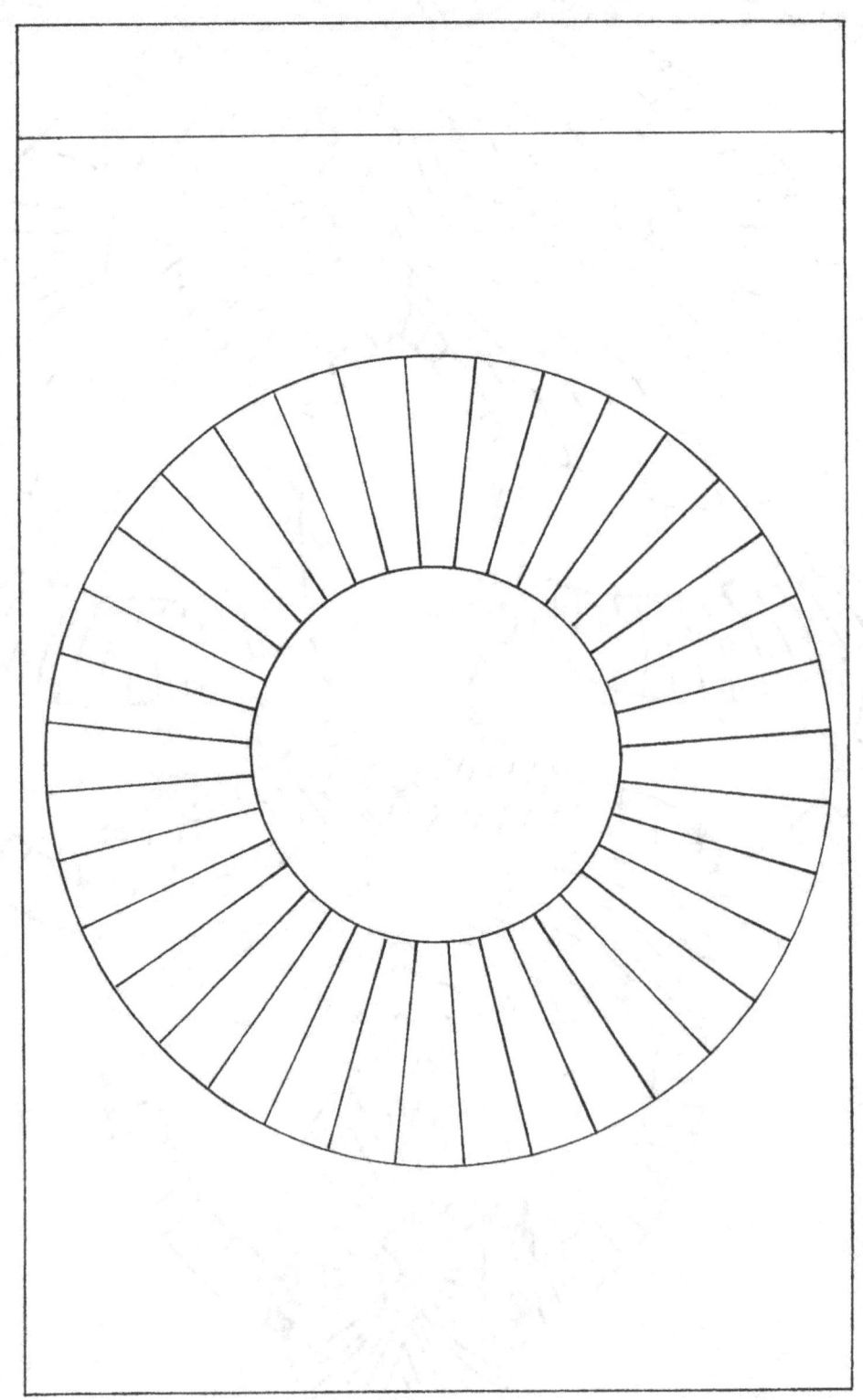

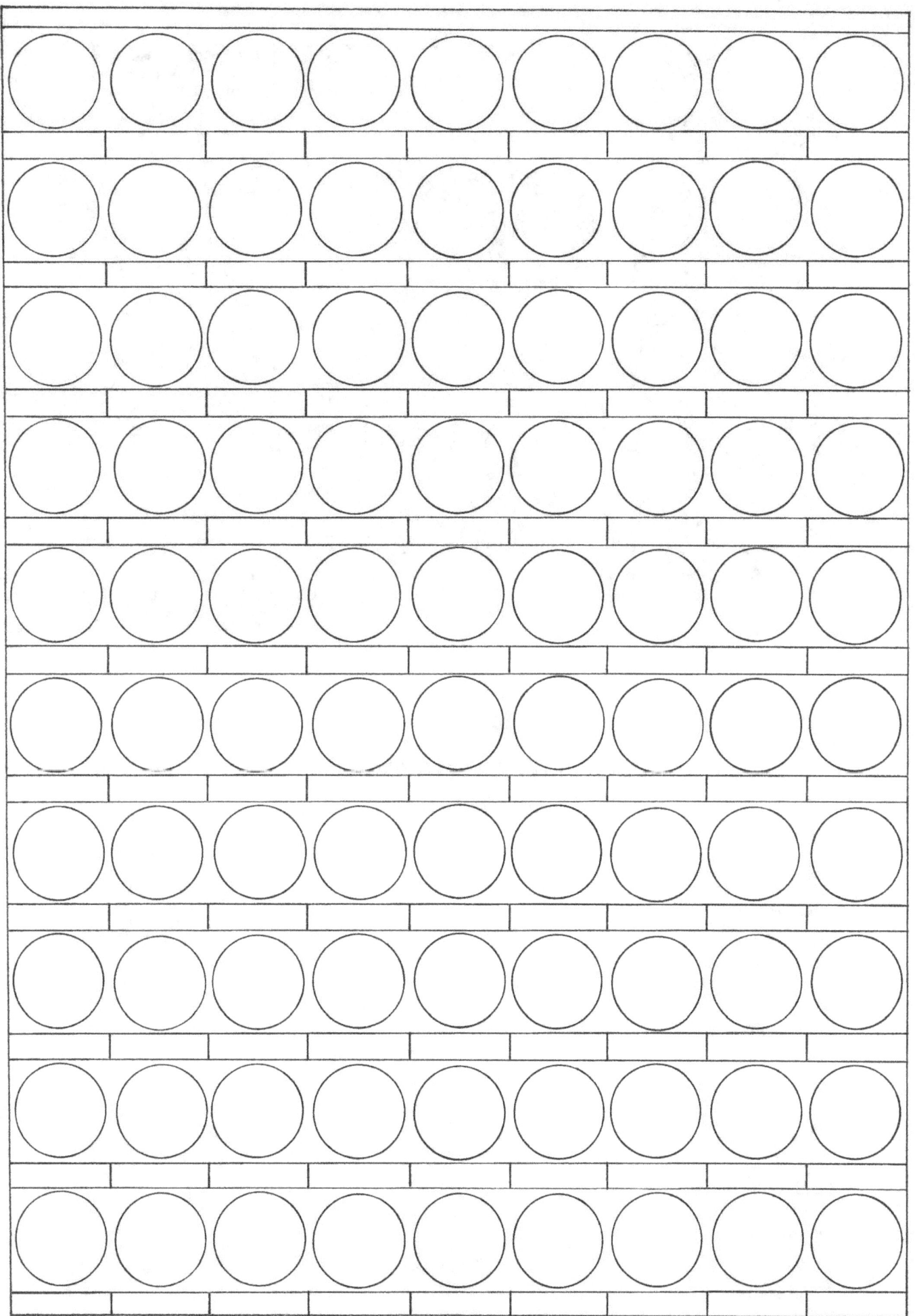

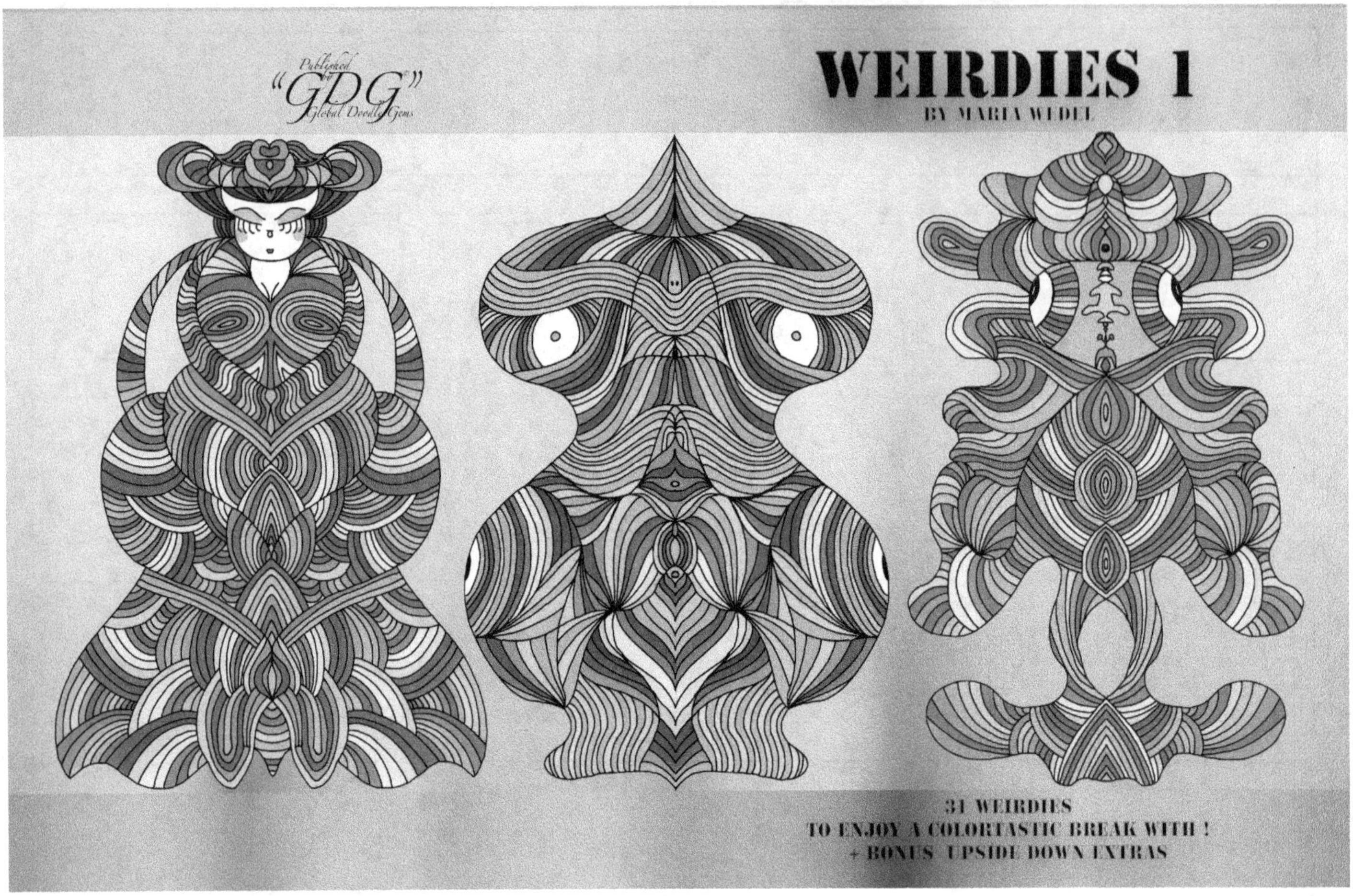

WEIRDIES 1
BY MARIA WEDEL

Published "GDG" Global Doodle Gems

**31 WEIRDIES
TO ENJOY A COLORTASTIC BREAK WITH!
+ BONUS UPSIDE DOWN EXTRAS**

*Check out
Weirdies 1
in the preview
of Weirdies 1*

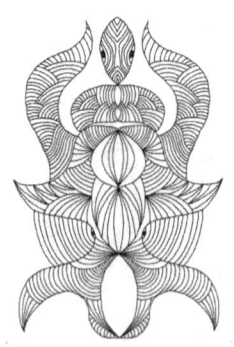
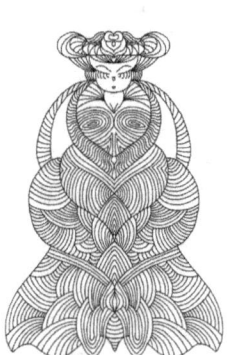
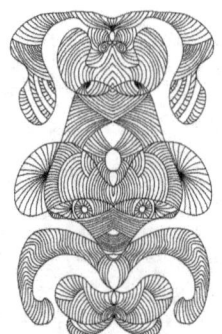
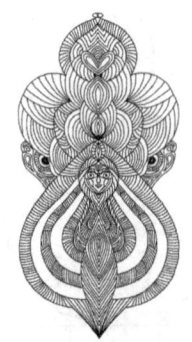
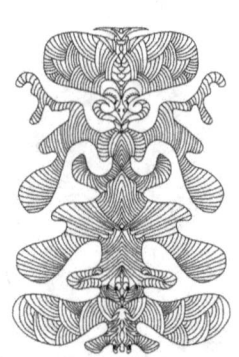

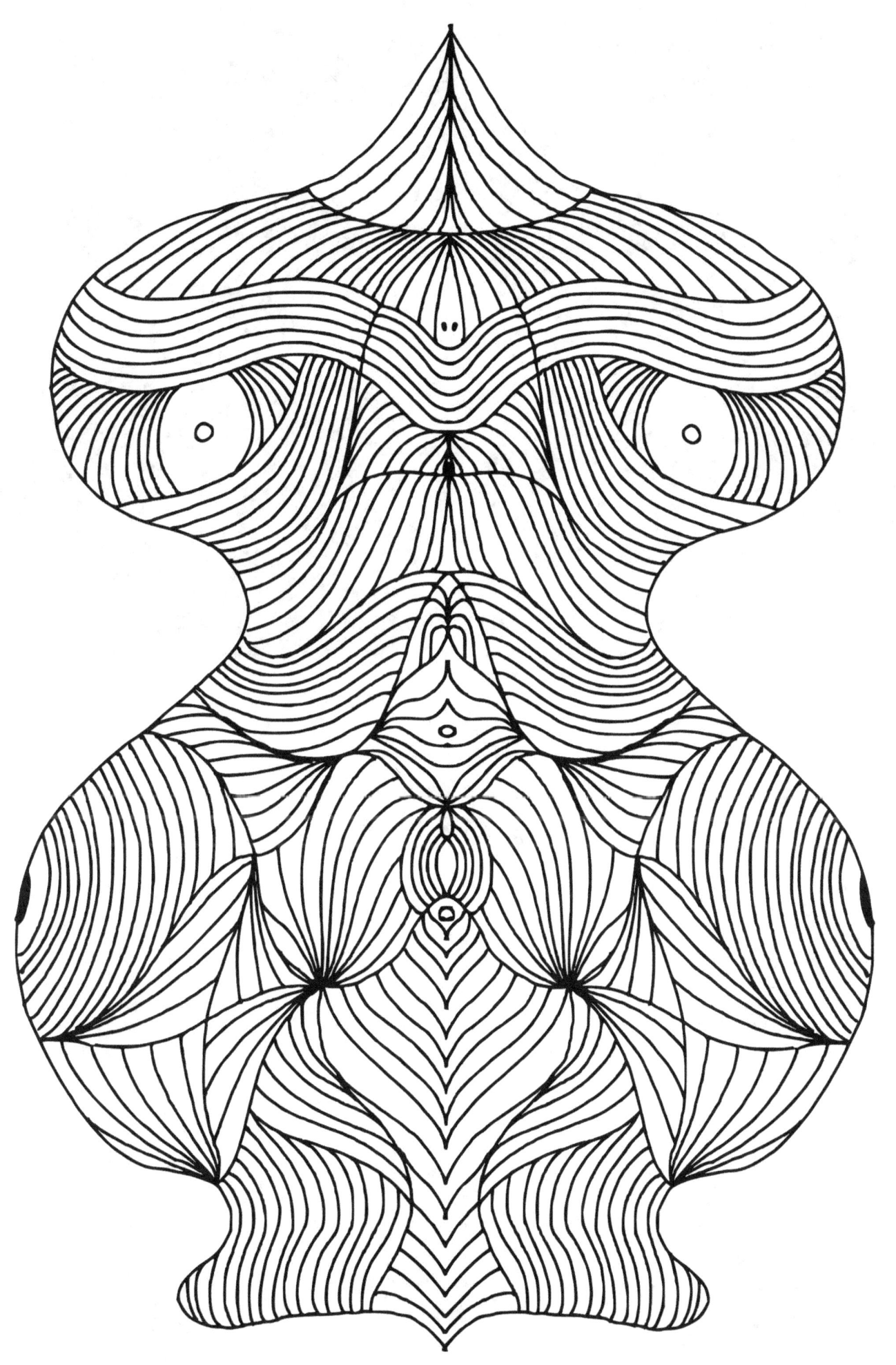

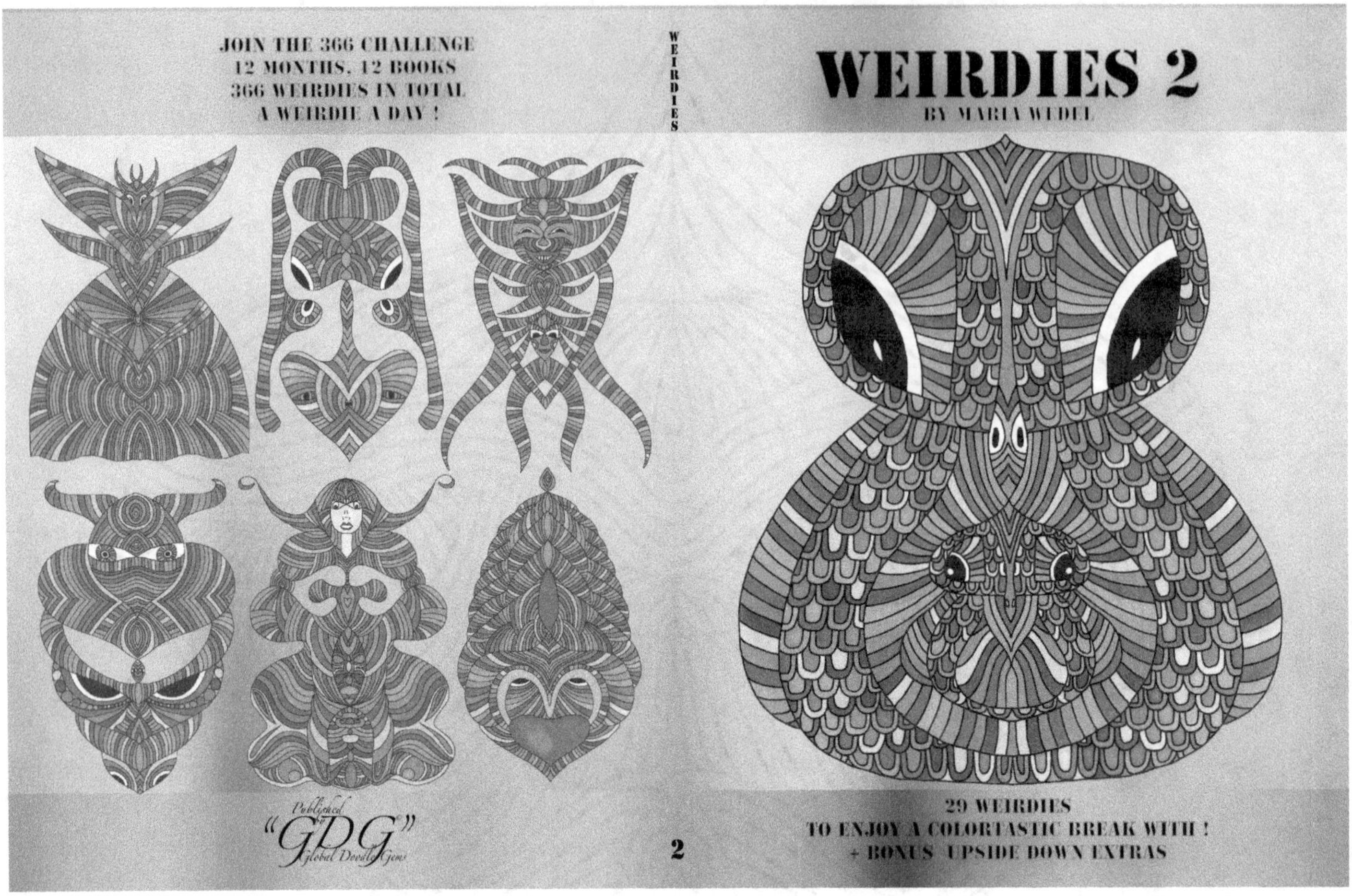

Check out
Weirdies 2
in the preview
of Weirdies 2

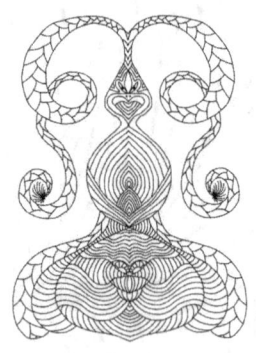
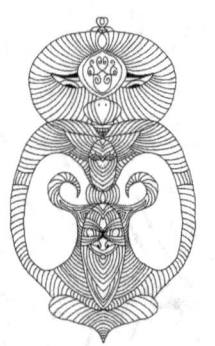
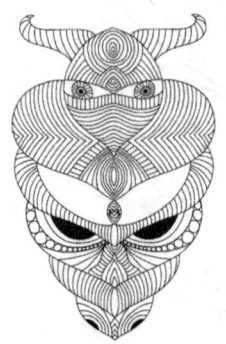
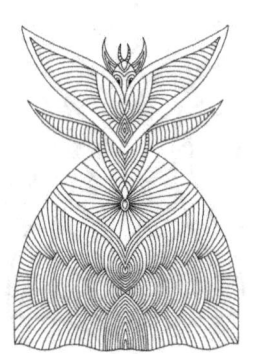
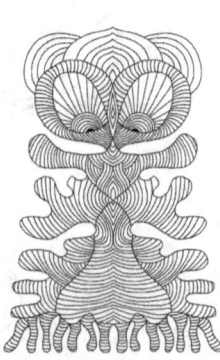

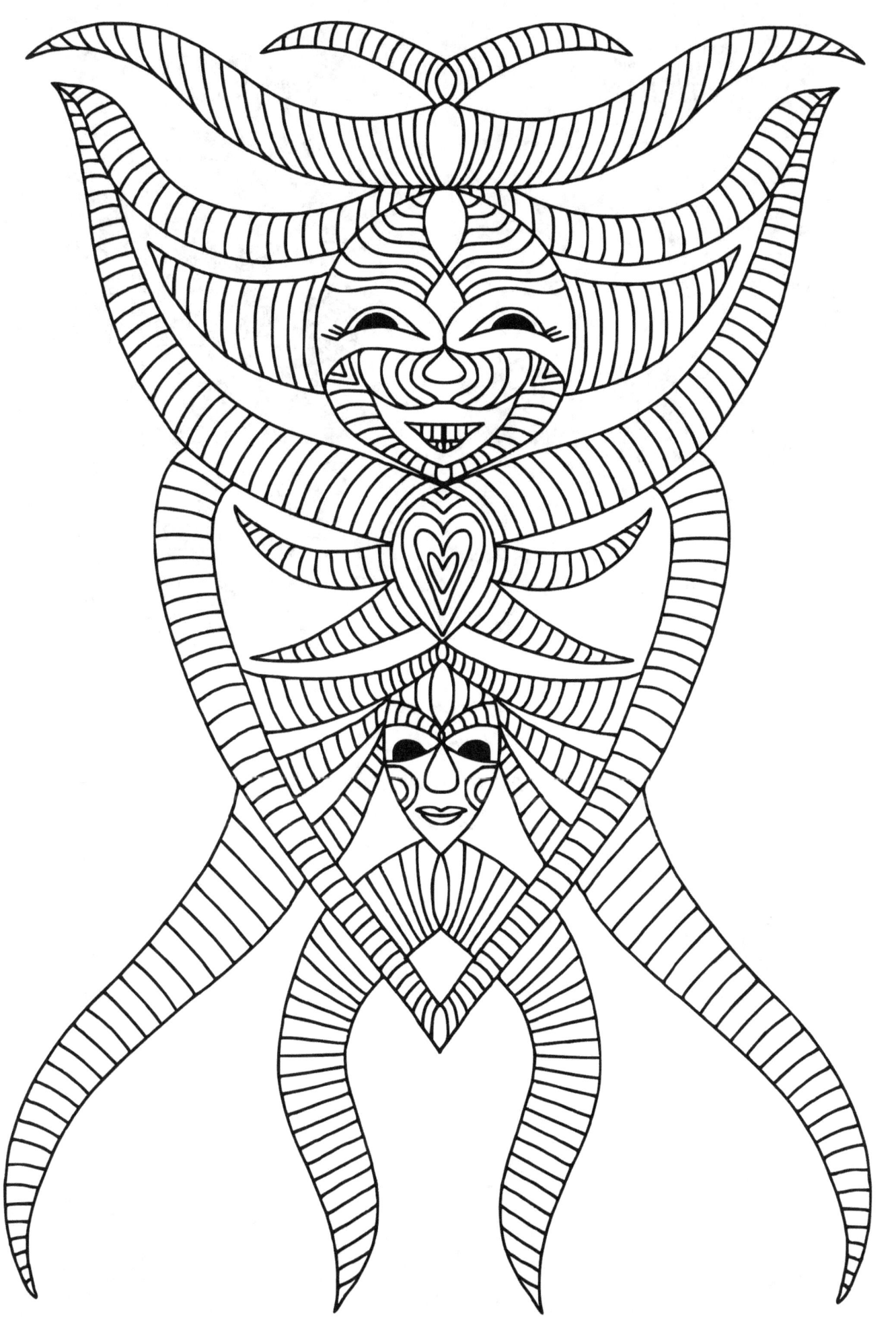

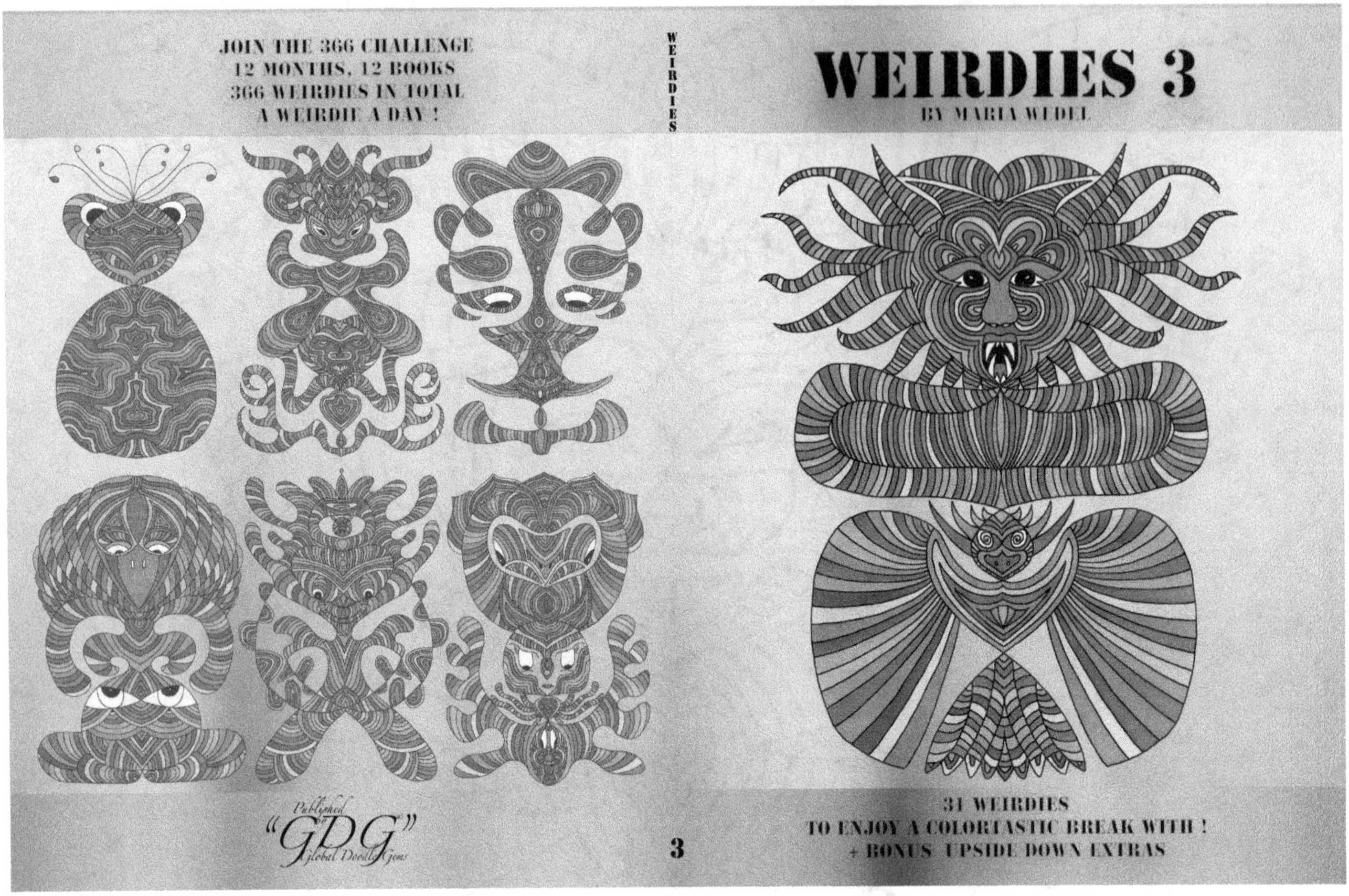

Check out
Weirdies 3
in the preview
of Weirdies 3

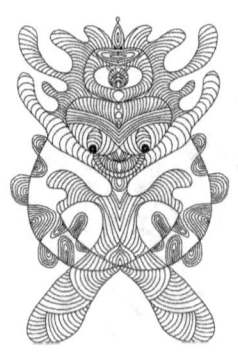
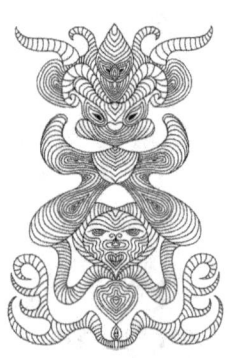
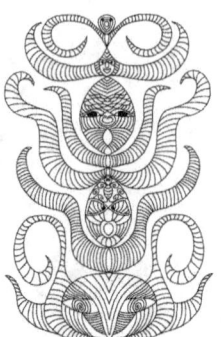
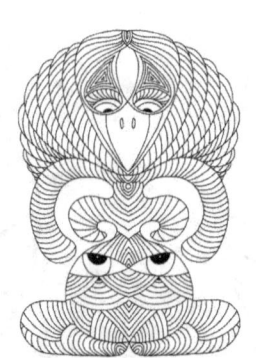
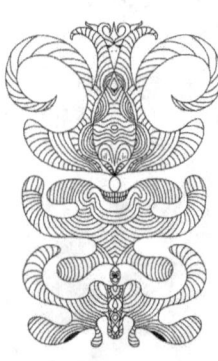

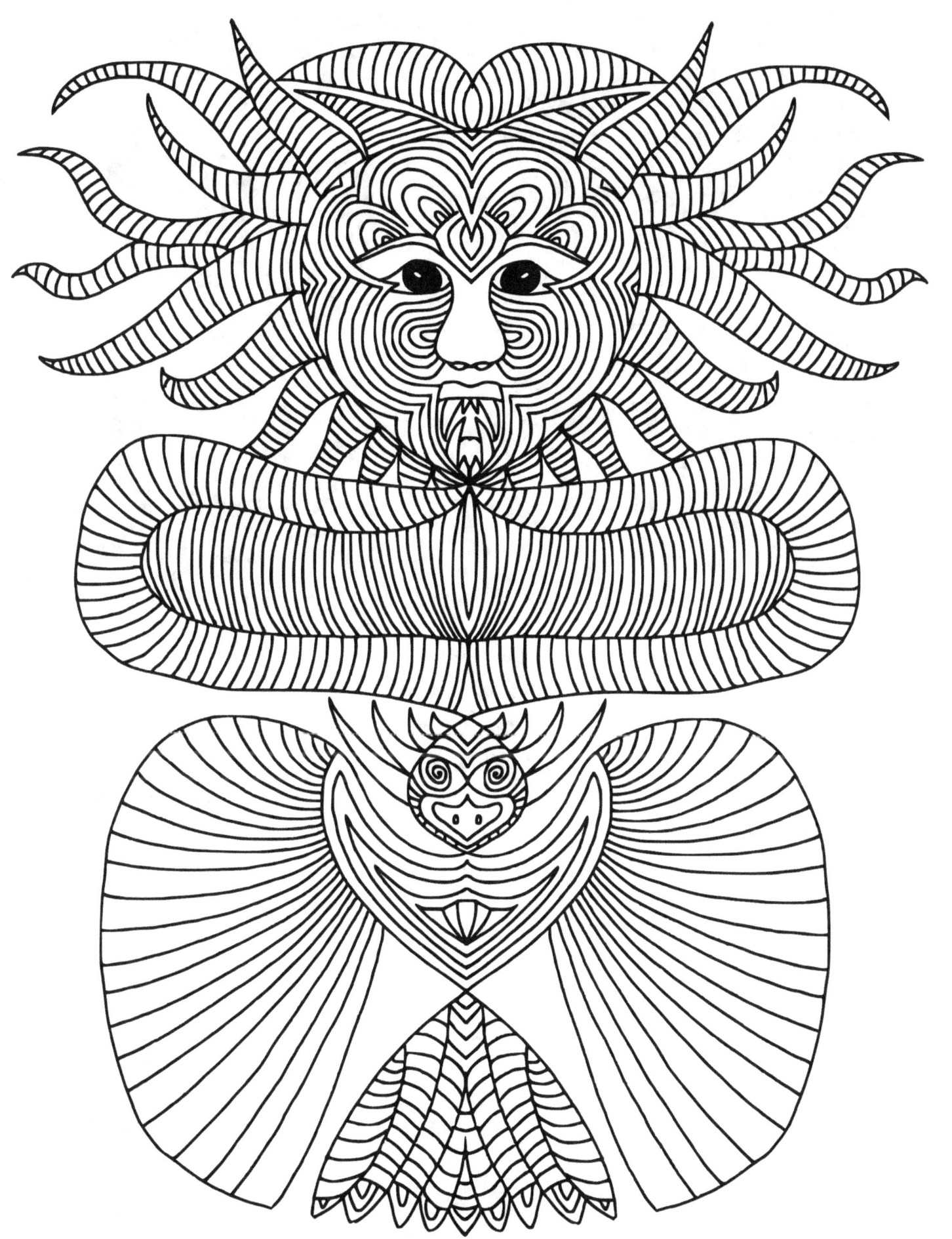

*Check out
Weirdies 4
in the preview
of Weirdies 4*

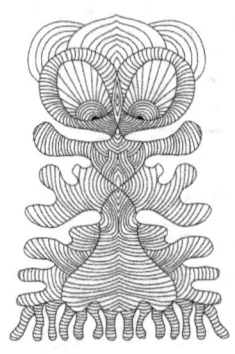
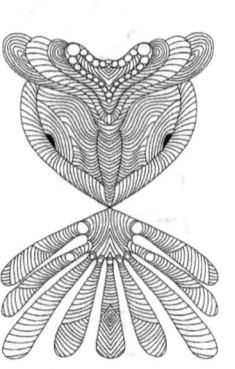
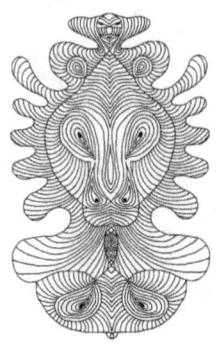
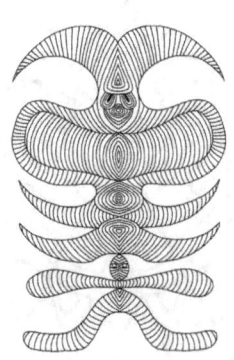
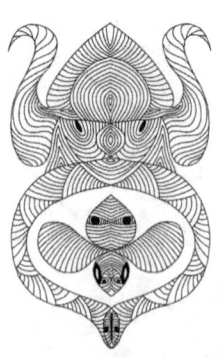

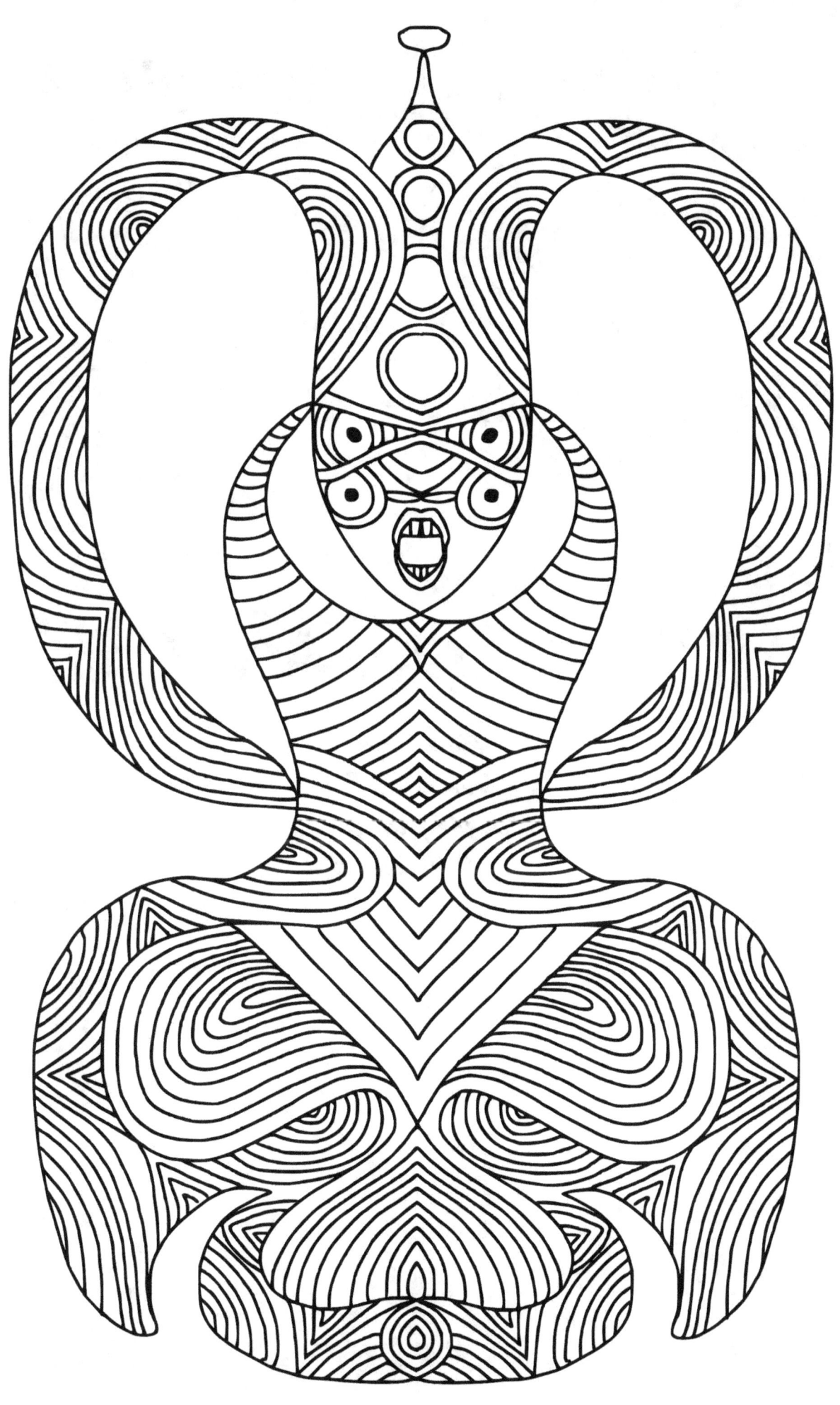

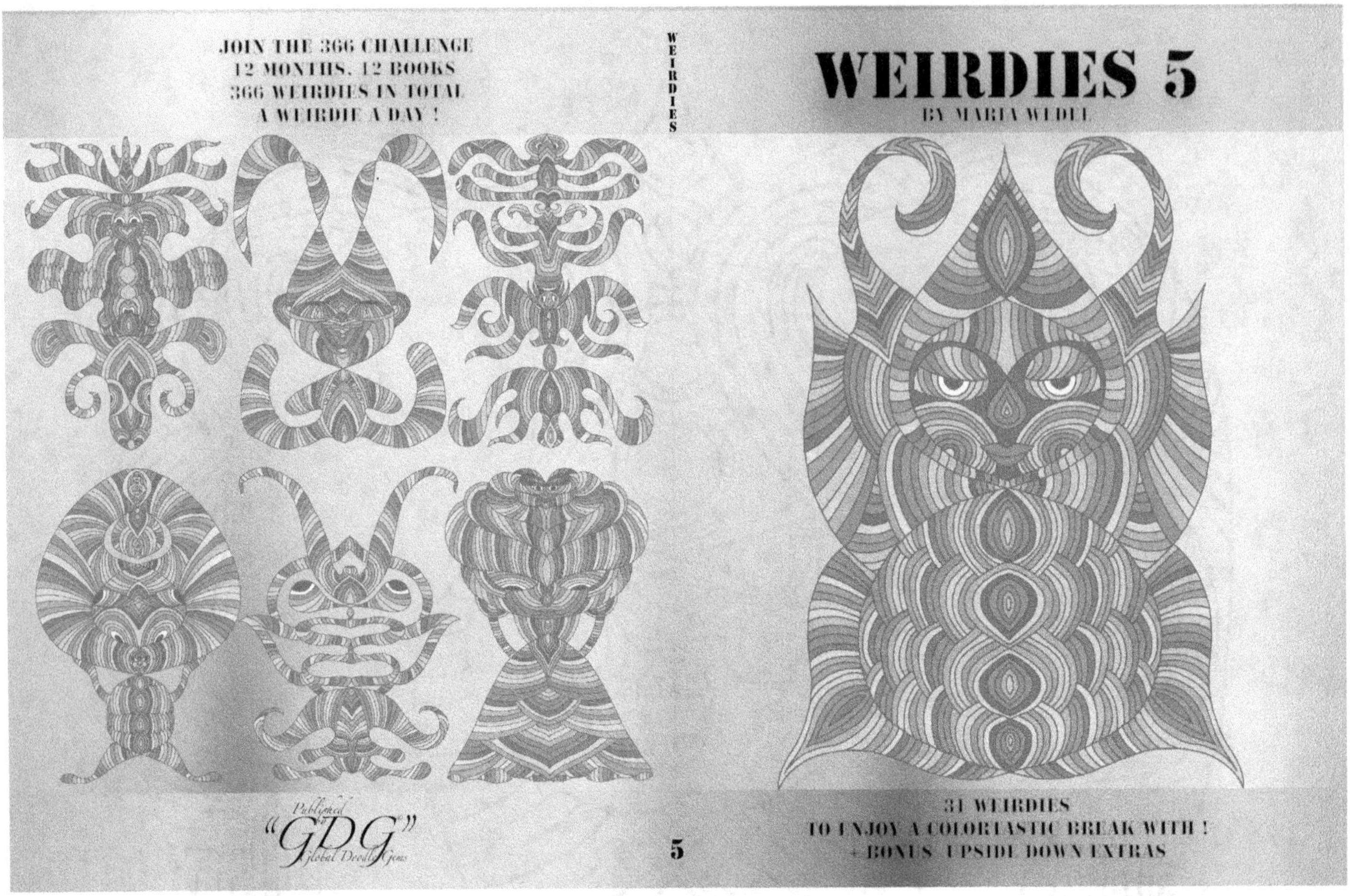

*Check out
Weirdies 5
in the preview
of Weirdies 5*

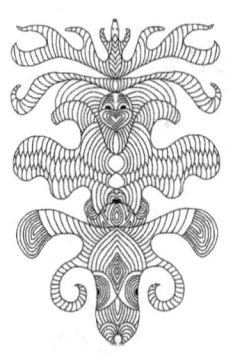
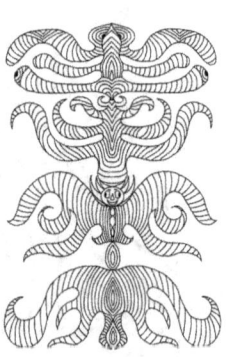
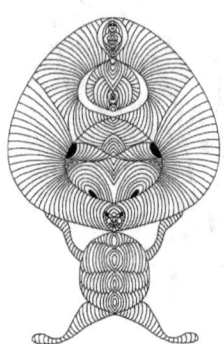
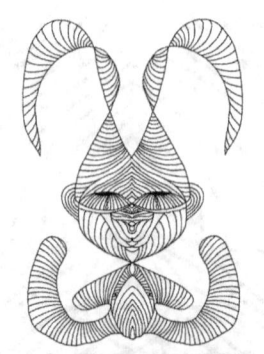
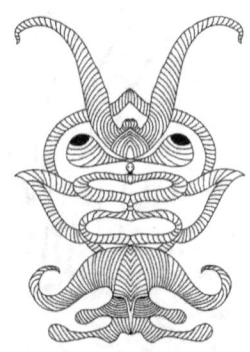

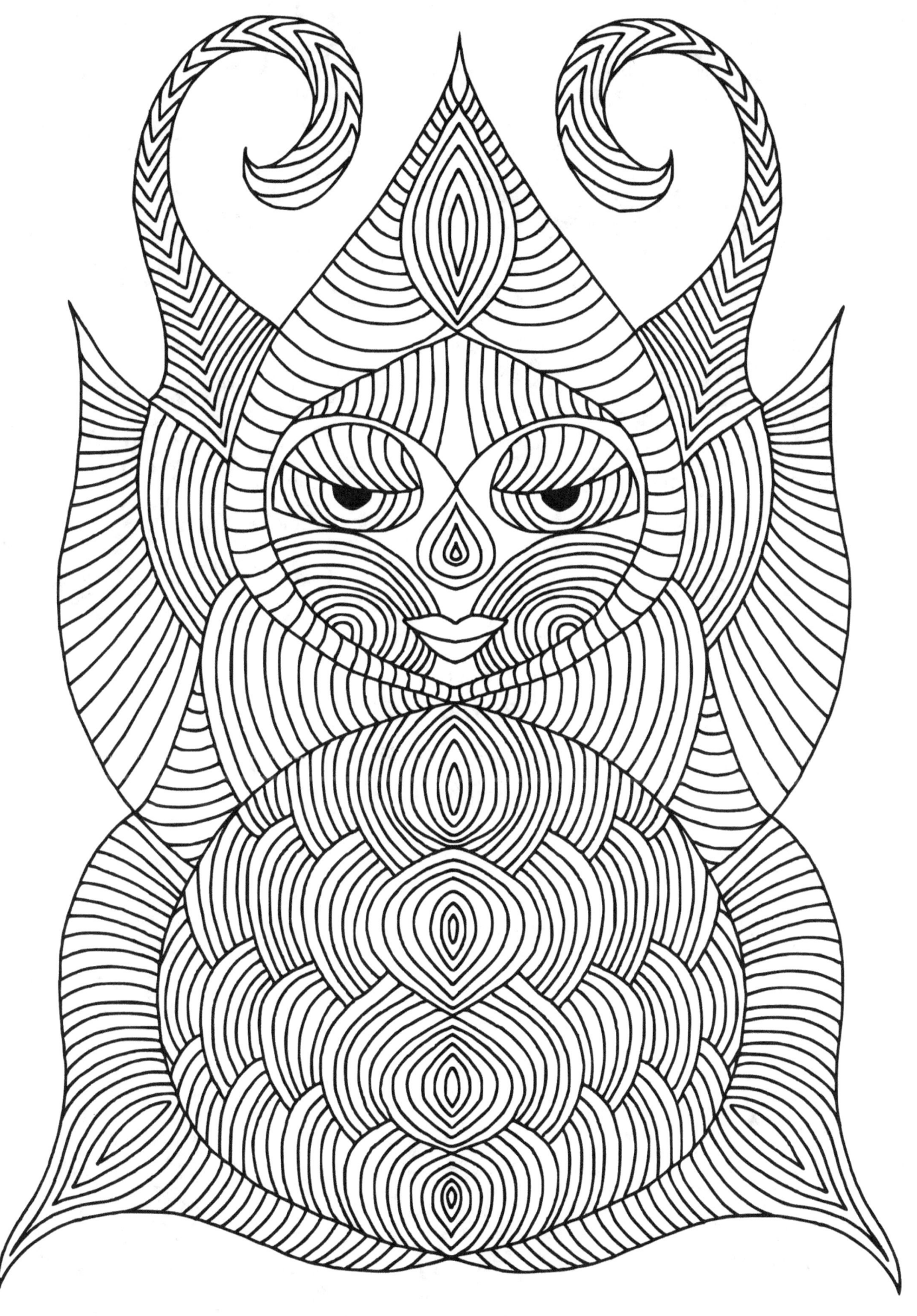

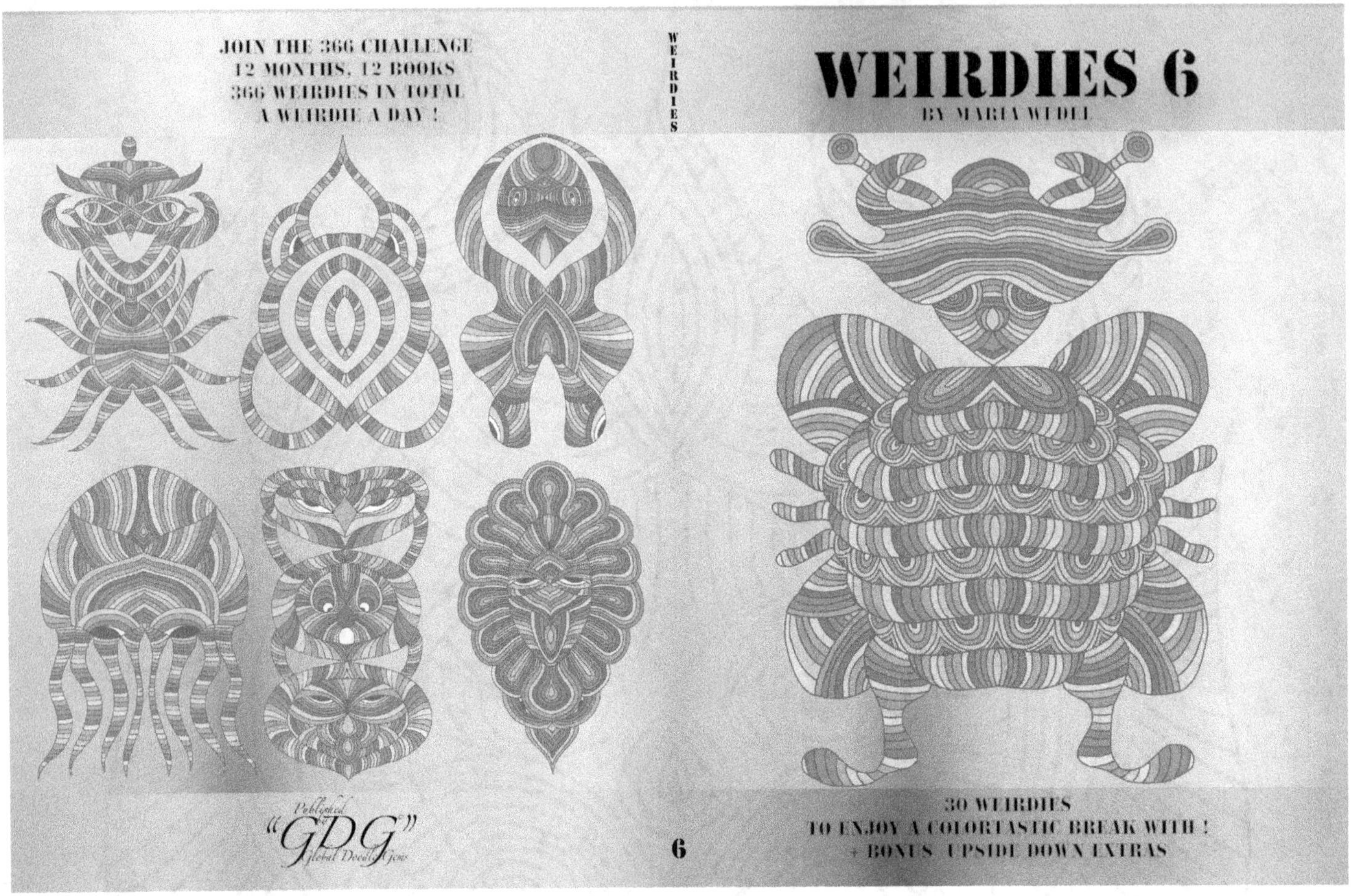

Check out
Weirdies 6
in the preview
of Weirdies 6

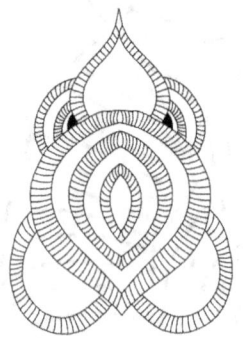
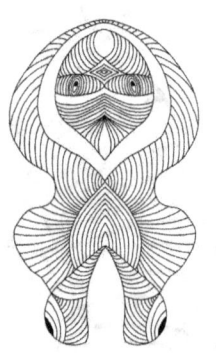
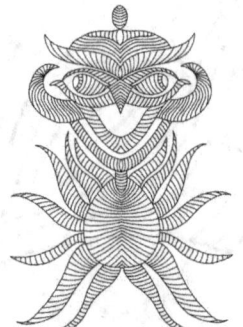
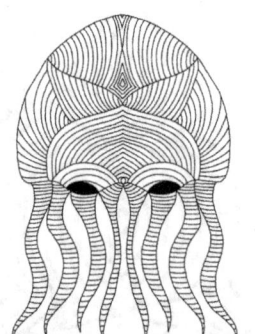
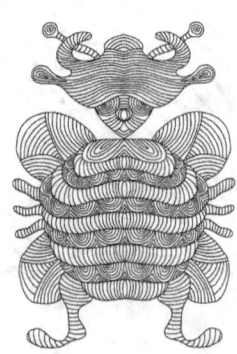

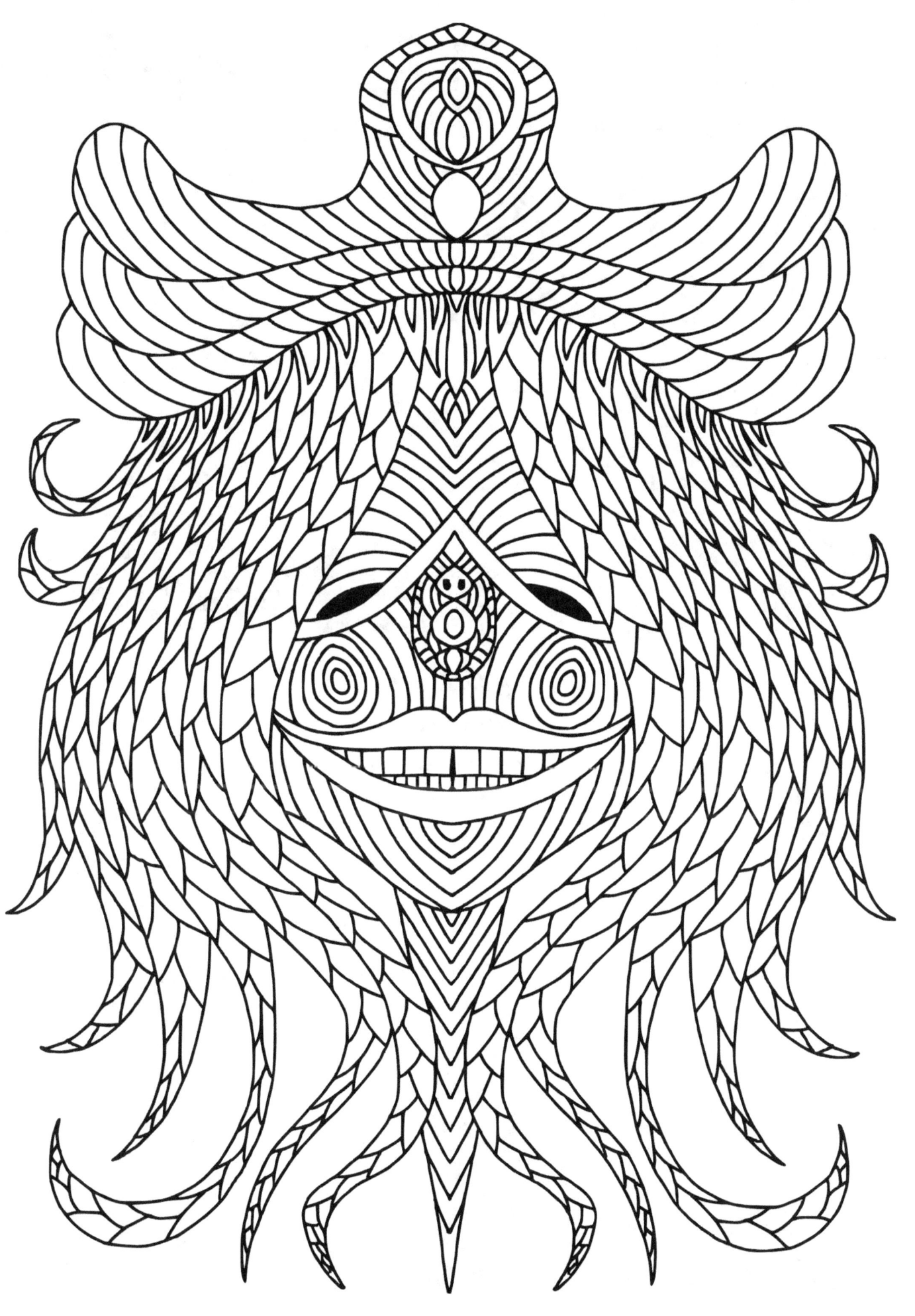

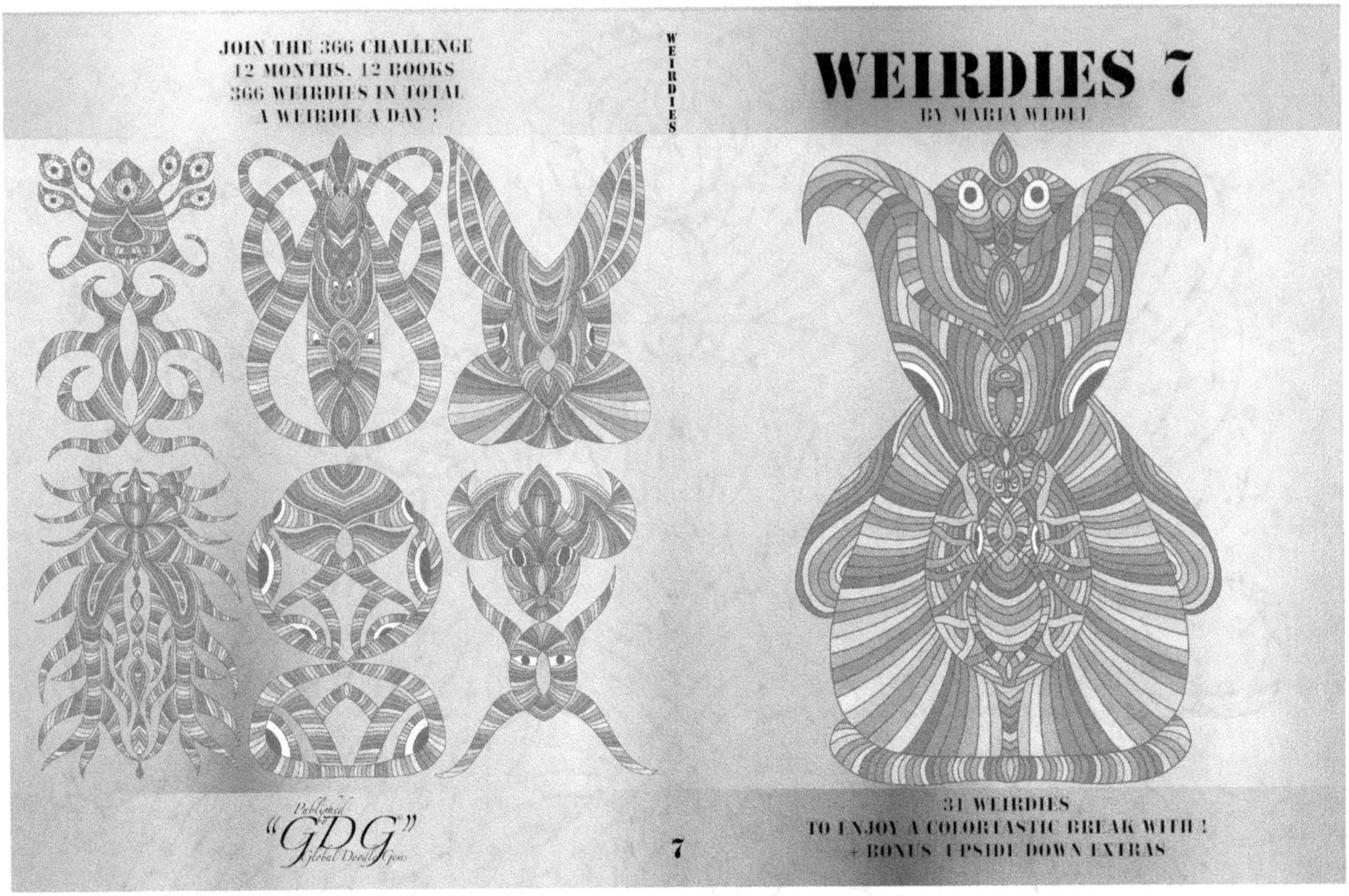

Check out
Weirdies 7
in the preview
of Weirdies 7

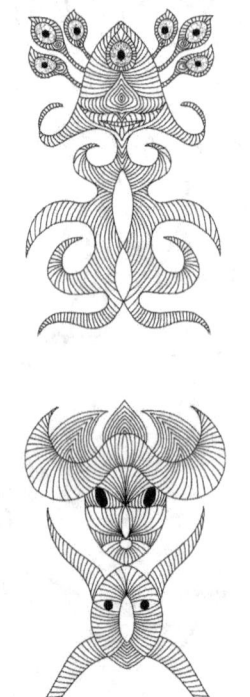
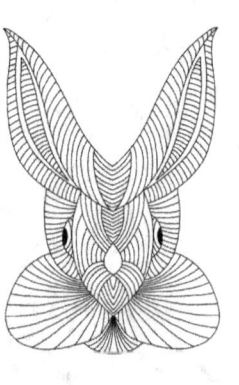
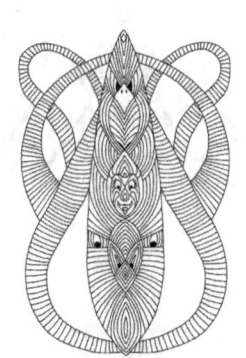
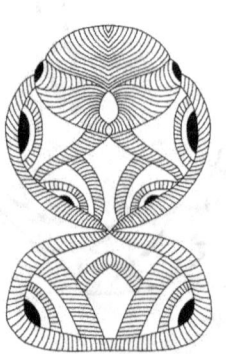

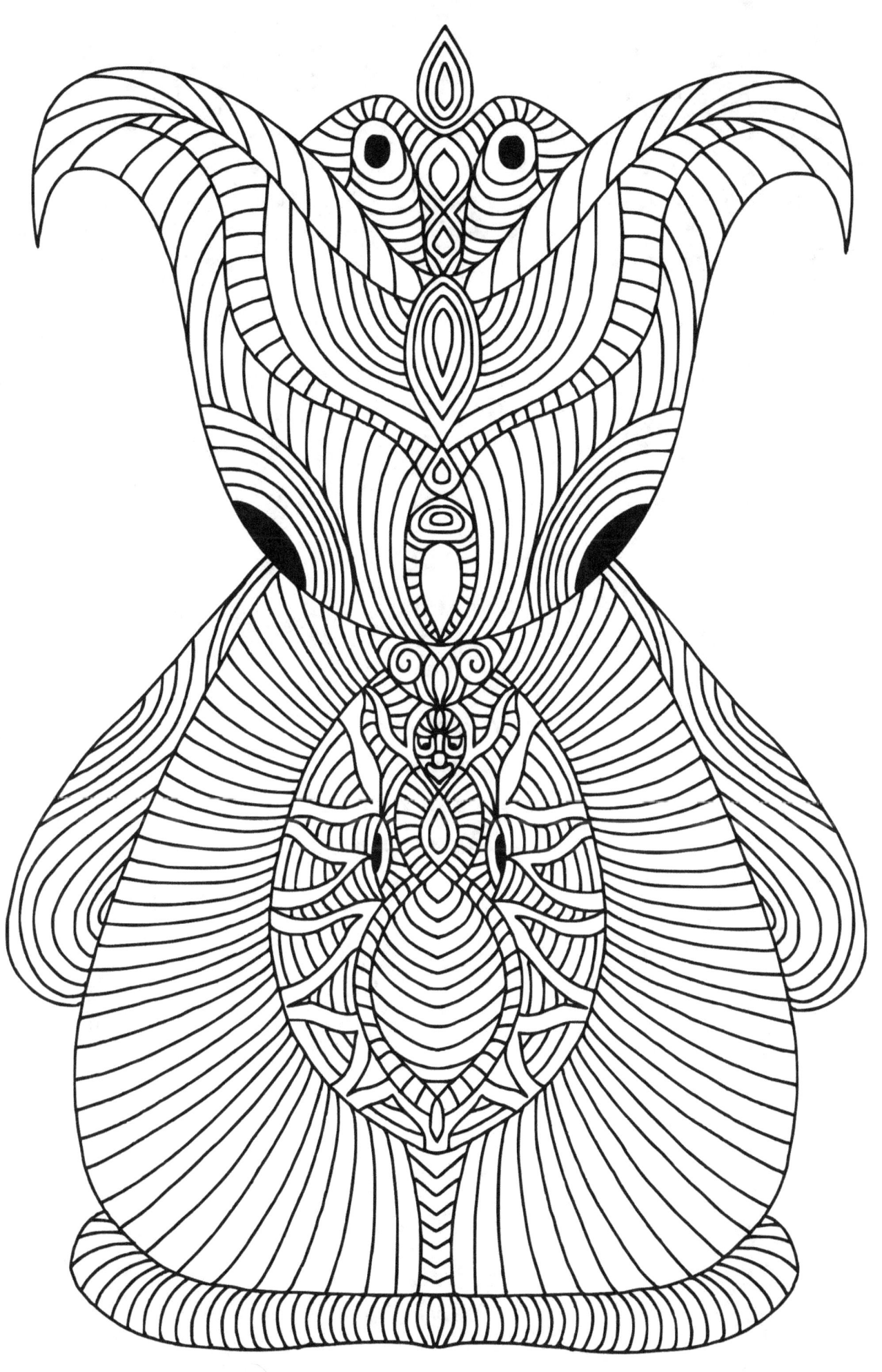

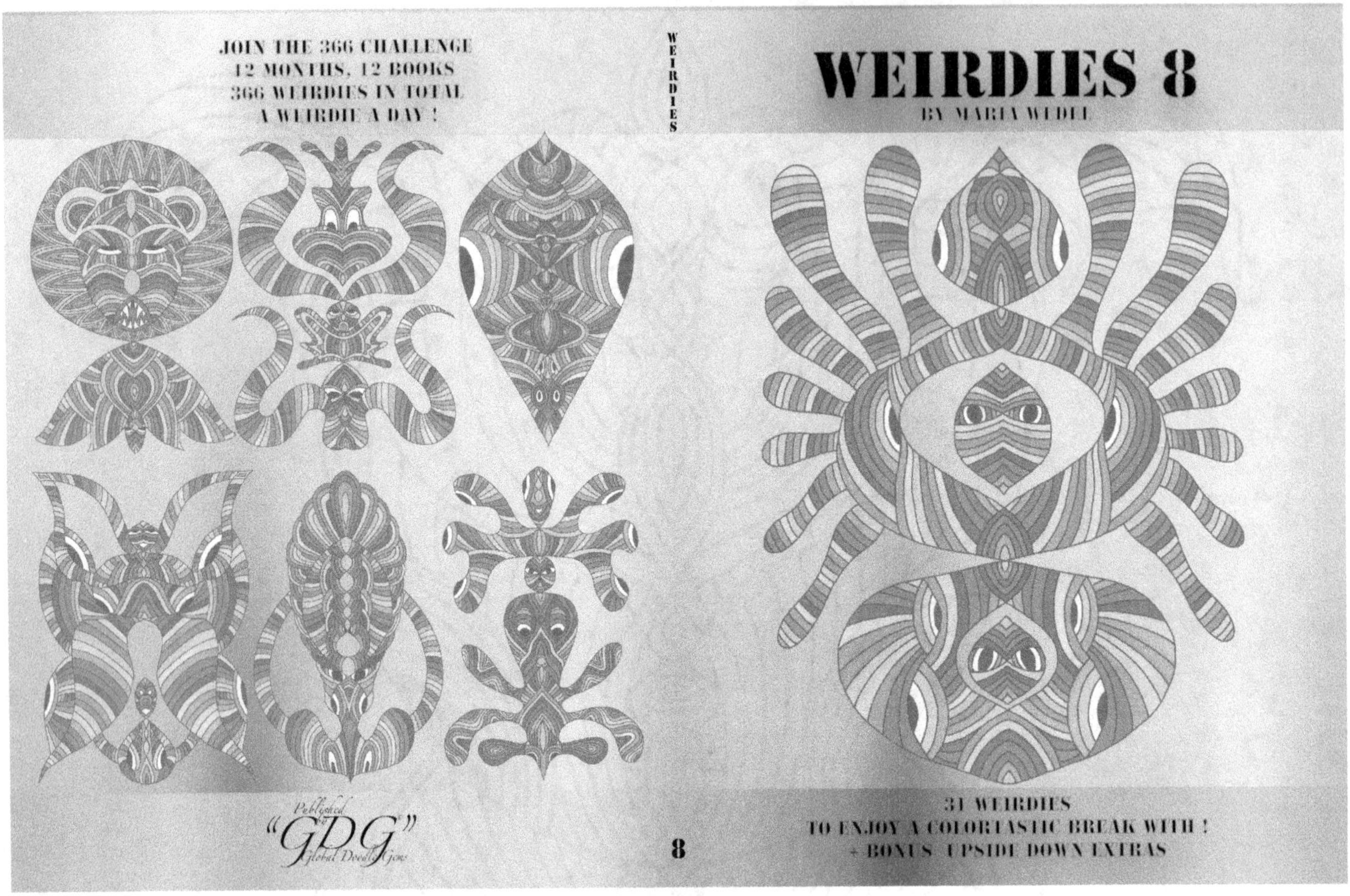

*Check out
Weirdies 8
in the preview
of Weirdies 8*

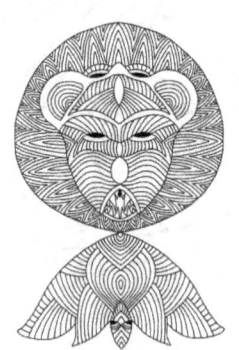
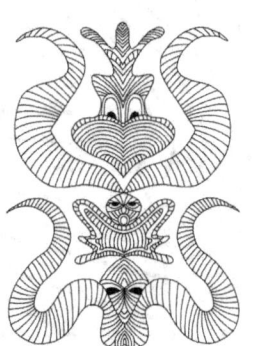
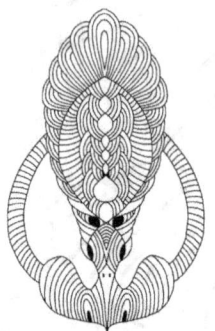
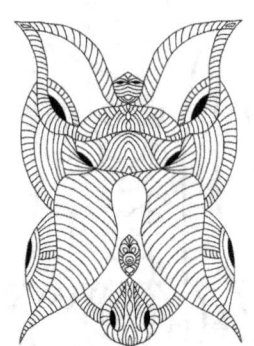
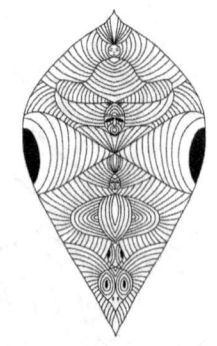

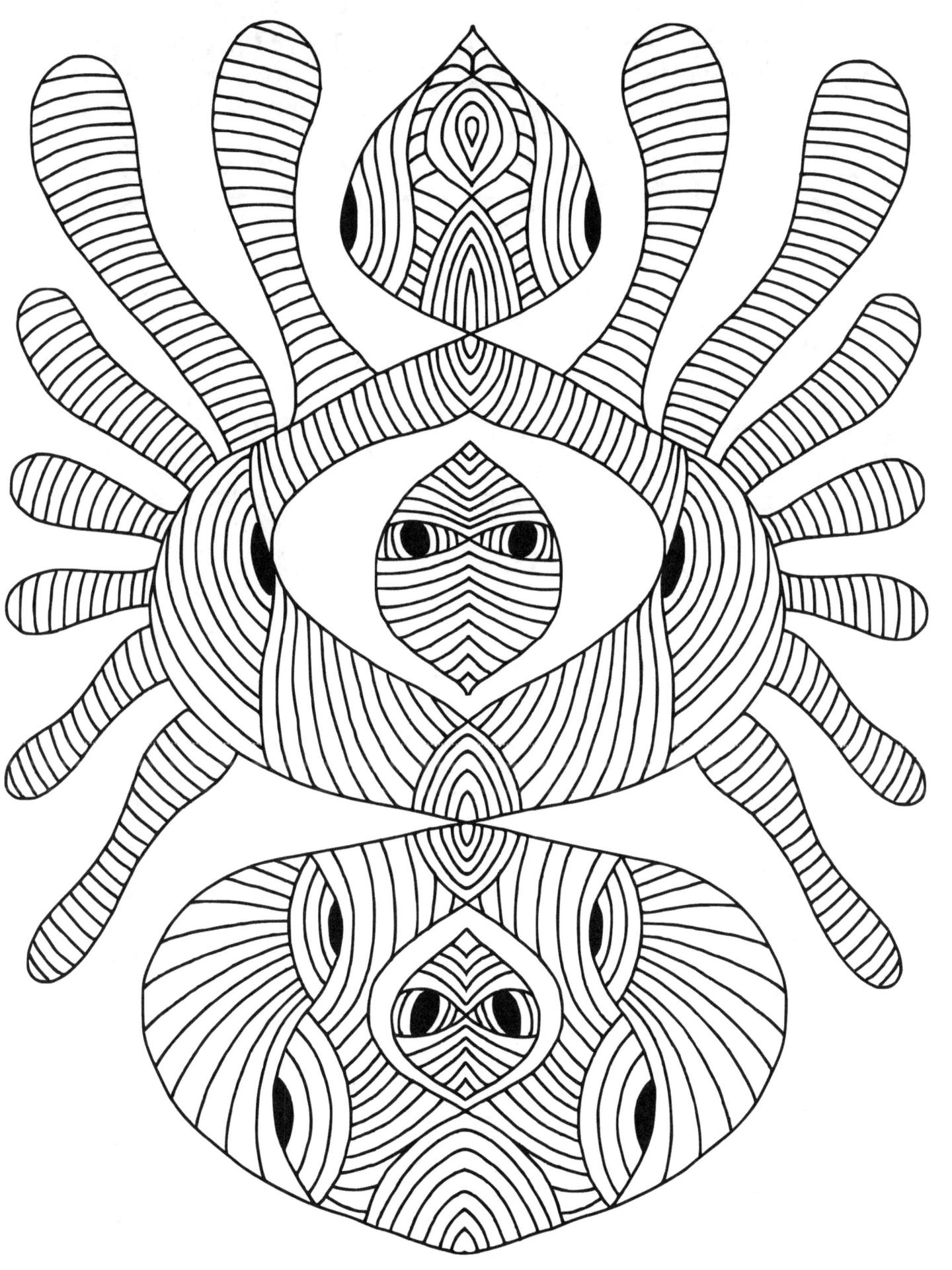

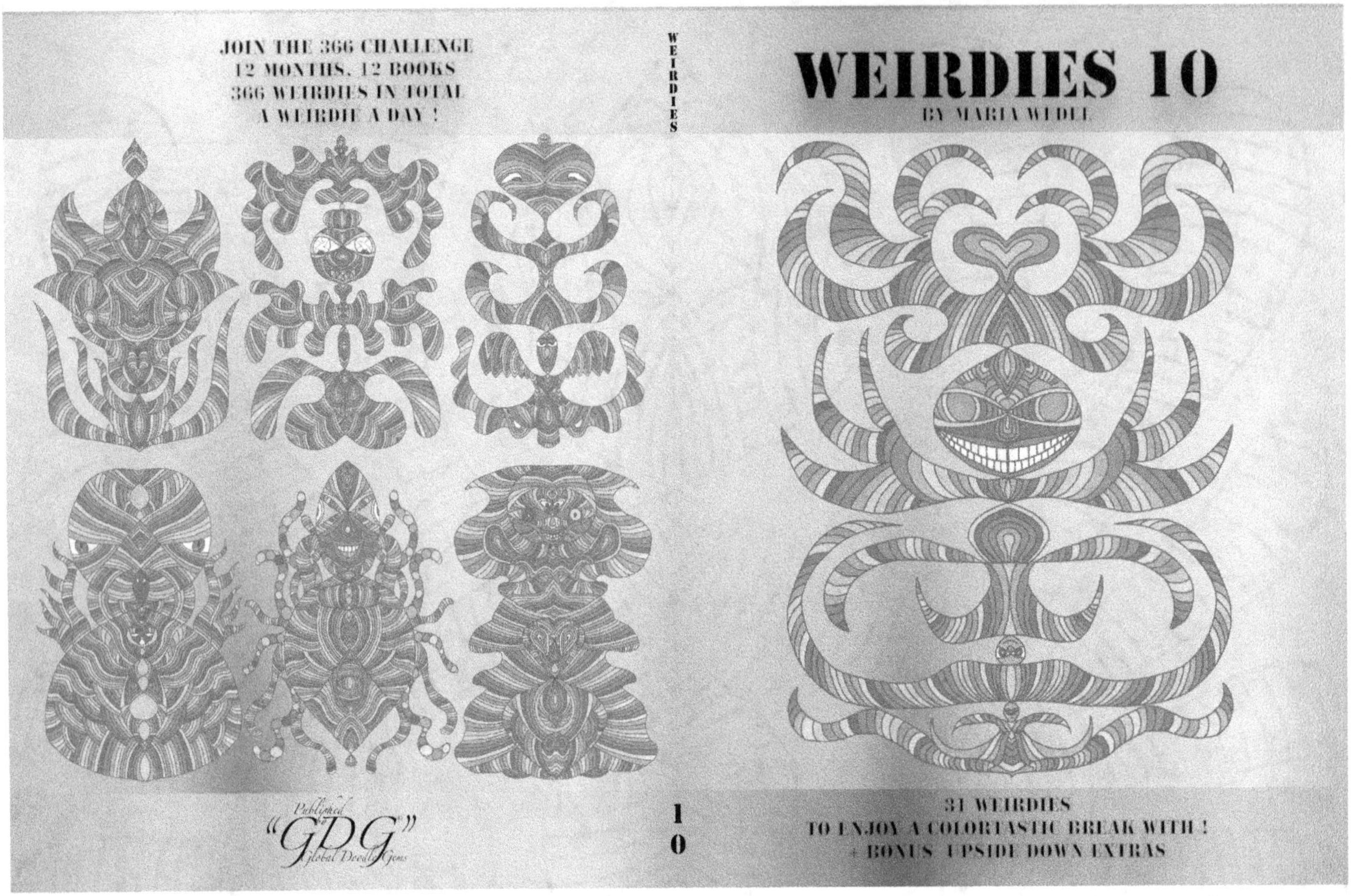

*Check out
Weirdies 8
in the preview
of Weirdies 8*

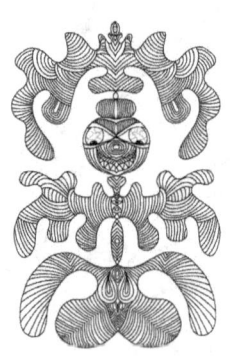
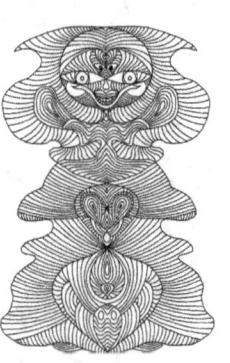
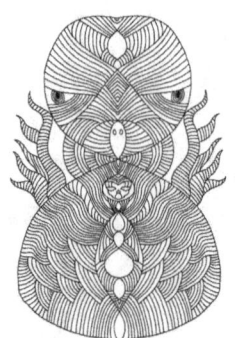
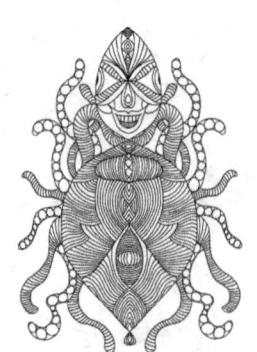
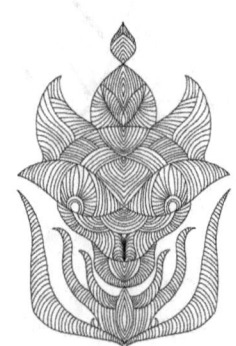

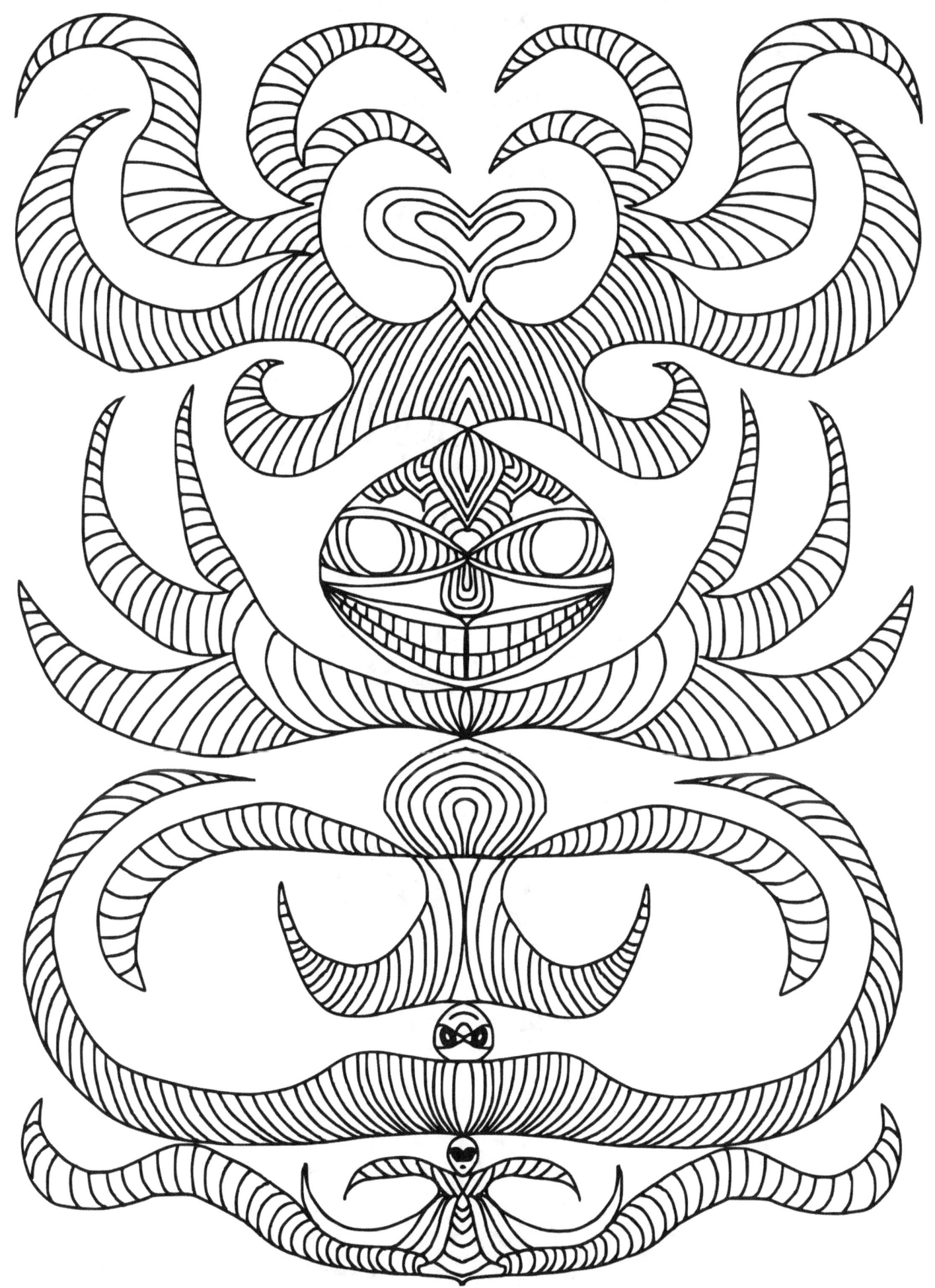

Other Titles by Maria Wedel

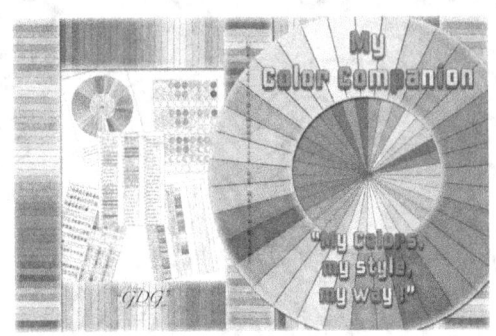

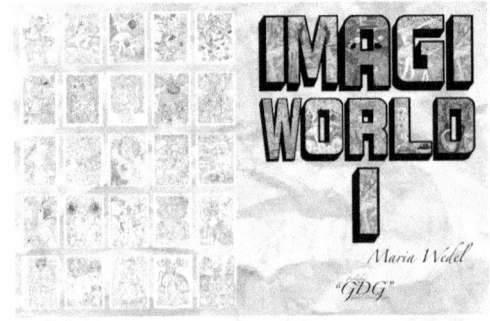

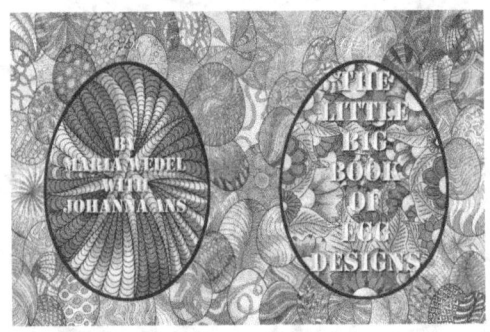

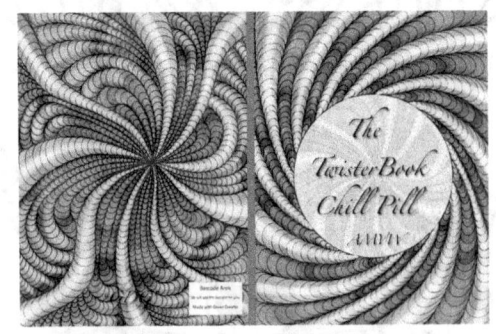

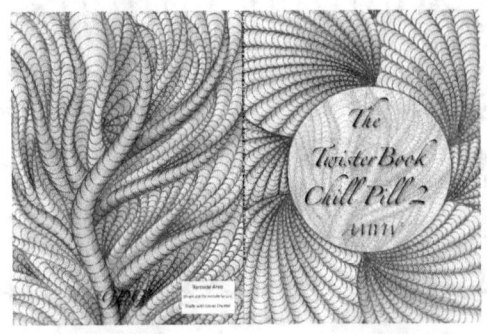

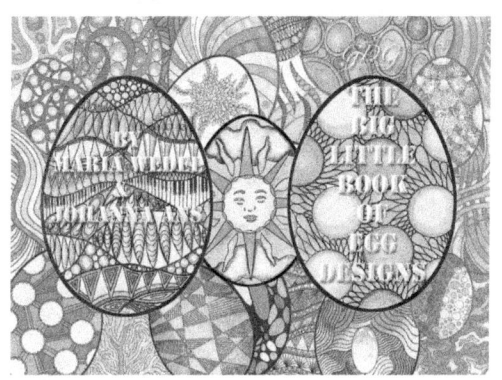
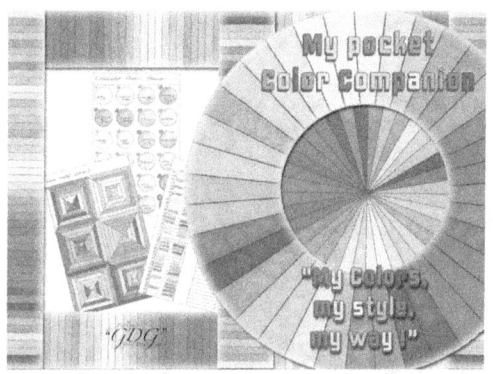
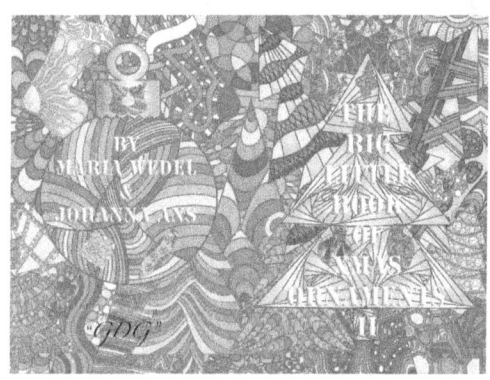
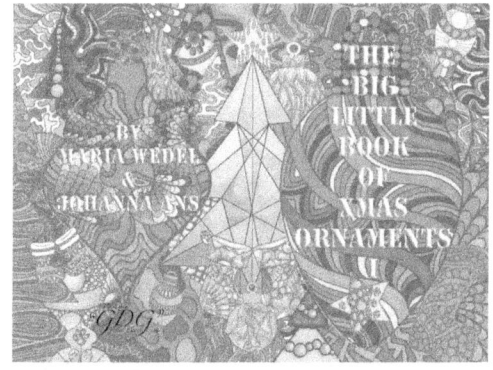
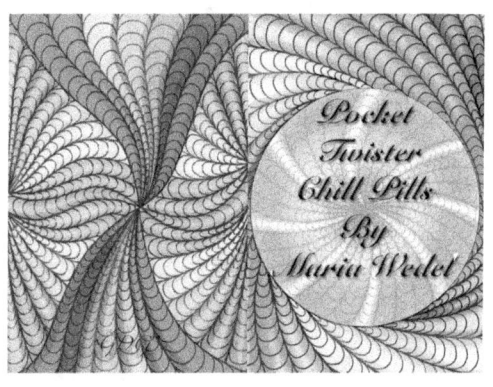

www.ingramcontent.com/pod-product-compliance
Lightning Source LLC
Chambersburg PA
CBHW082333220526
45470CB00008B/2490